THE IDEOLOGY OF
PEACE

The author, third from left, planting an olive tree in Jerusalem during a peace conference of all religions in 1995.

THE IDEOLOGY OF
PEACE

TOWARDS A CULTURE OF PEACE

Maulana Wahiduddin Khan

Goodword Books

Translated by
Farida Khanam

First published 2003
© Goodword Books 2003

Goodword Books Pvt. Ltd.
1, Nizamuddin West Market
New Delhi-110 013
Tel. +9111–4355454, 4356666
Fax +9111–4357333, 4357980
e-mail: info@goodwordbooks.com
www.goodwordbooks.com

CONTENTS

FOREWORD

PEACE for me is not just an academic subject. It is the goal of my existence. I have dreamt of peace for as long as I can remember. I can truthfully say of myself that I am a born pacifist, and leading a peace-loving life has always been a source of great spiritual solace for me. In short, the mission of my life may be called a peace mission.

By nature, I have always been a vegetarian. Killing and violence are simply abhorrent to my inborn nature. I feel that such acts are perhaps incompatible with my genetic code. Perhaps I was born with such a nature as would make me feel highly sensitive on this matter, so that I might recognize its importance and play my part to the full in this peace mission.

I have been acknowledged throughout my life as a peaceful and non-violent person. Indeed, any incident of violence so greatly agitates me that the tears spring to my eyes, whether it takes place at home or abroad, and whether the victims are known or unknown to me. There have been many such incidents in my life. I would like to recount one of them to illustrate my point.

Once, in the days of my youth, my elder brother set off along with his friends to go hunting. He insisted that I should go along too, so I had no option but to join him.

We left in two cars, and after about two hours' drive, we passed through the outskirts of the city and came to fields and orchards. Now my brother and his friends started hunting birds perched high up in the trees. Then they handed a gun to me and asked me to fire at a bird (*kahlak*) sitting at the top of a tree.

I did as they asked, took the gun, placed it against my shoulder and aimed at the bird. But when the bird came exactly within range, I had such a feeling of unease that I could not bring myself to pull the trigger. I handed the gun back to my brother. My heart was so heavy that I immediately took leave of my brothers and cousins, walked some distance on foot and then took a bus back home to Allahabad.

I am a pacifist, but my pacifism is not of a strategic nature. It is not a formula for justifying support in one case or opposition in another. My pacifism extends to all of humanity. It has positive value in the full sense of the word. My pacifism is an absolute good, it has the status of a summum bonum for me. It is not simply a theory. It is a part of my flesh and blood. It is the pain of my heart. It is my life. It is the voice of my soul. I have watered the plant of peace with my tears. I have lived for the cause of peace for the whole of my life and I finally want to die for the cause of peace.

The public phase of my peace mission started on 28 February, 1955, when a public meeting was held in the historic city of Lucknow. I made a speech on that occasion, which began with these words: "We stand at the threshold of a new era. Future historians will call it the atomic age, but perhaps no historian will survive to tell the tale of the destruction of humanity." This speech was published in 1955 in the form of a pamphlet titled: *On the Threshold of a New Era*.

After the second world war, the succeeding half century had cast a gloom upon it by the danger of atomic war. However, it is a matter of great satisfaction that we have now stepped into the twenty-first century with the hope that the danger of atomic war has almost been averted, and that a new age of peace has set in all over the world.

The present book is a gift to the new generation from a peace-loving person. It attempts to present a complete ideology of life based on peace, which can be summed up in these words: Peace is not an option: it is our destiny.

We shall either live with peace or destroy ourselves without it. In this world it is undeniable that the future is for peace alone. There is no future for war or violence.

Wahiduddin Khan

New Delhi
July 19, 2002

THE IDEOLOGY OF PEACE

HISTORY abounds in preachers of peace. But it is hard to find in its annals an ideologue who has been capable of presenting the concept of peace as a complete ideology. Perhaps this is why over the centuries no revolution in the true sense of the word has been brought about on the basis of peace. Although we have had a number of peace-loving individuals, the establishment of a peaceful society on a mass scale has never become a reality. Human interests have been very deeply associated with peace. That is why every individual, for personal reasons, wants to have a peaceful life.

But he is repeatedly faced with such diverse situations that he needs an ideology of peace to guide him. For peace being the human need is not enough to make him exercise restraint and remain peaceable in all situations. He needs an ideology which convinces him *at the conscious level* of the necessity to keep the peace at all times.

We can find examples of this in human history. For instance, let's take democracy. Man has always instinctively cherished the idea of a democratic polity and we find some instances in human history where such a system had been successfully established, although only in a partial way. But the advent of a full-fledged revolution on the basis of democracy became a reality only when the thinkers of modern Europe presented the instinctive aspirations of human beings in the form of a comprehensive ideology.

The same is the case with peace. Peace has always been, in every age, a human need. However, in modern times, peace has become so vital to the survival of mankind that it has now literally become a matter of life and death for humanity. Peace means life: its absence means death.

The writer's aim is to present peace in the form of a complete ideology—an ideology which awakens human consciousness; which provides the answer to all life's problems in terms of peace; which describes the utmost importance of peace, right from the individual to the international level. Peace is a prerequisite for all kinds of human progress. With peace, we progress: without peace, we face ruin.

Why should an ideology be required for peace? There are two principal reasons for this. When one focuses on an objective, one has to adopt one factor and discard another. This can be done with conviction only when one has clear and specific theoretical justification for it. Without this, one cannot be wholehearted in one's acceptance or rejection of any concept or practice. For instance, if the notion takes root in the minds of certain individuals that their rights have been usurped and that to redress their grievances they must resort to violence, it will be impossible to dissuade them, unless we are able to prove with forceful arguments that violence is not the solution to their problems, that such a course will only aggravate matters and will never restore to them their rights. To bring these individuals to the path of peace, it is essential that they should be convinced by an ideology based on reason that, to achieve their objectives, they must essentially renounce violent methods and conduct their struggle along peaceful lines. Ideology gives us the logical basis as to why one course of action should be rejected and another course of action should be adopted.

Man can properly fulfill any given mission only when he is ideologically convinced of its validity. Ideology provides man with the necessary warranties, otherwise he fails to act with the necessary energy and enthusiasm so vital to the success of any struggle.

In similar vein, courage is the greatest energizer in the journey of life. A courageous man can climb to the top of a mountain, whereas a man devoid of courage cannot even proceed along level pathways. But what is man's source of courage? It is ideology which provides man with the courage to tread the path of peace. It has been rightly said that "Man is a rational animal" and also that "man is an explanation-seeking animal." Both these sayings convey the same point: that man derives mental satisfaction from his actions only when the goals at which they are aimed have been established as right by rational argument. Attempting to evolve a complete ideology on the basis of peace is indeed as important a goal as peace itself, and vice versa. Both are interdependent. The one cannot exist without the other.

Such violence as has been witnessed in modern times has never hitherto been experienced. Wartime depredations and violence by unauthorized groups in the form of proxy or guerilla warfare have inflicted such great harm upon humanity that this seems to be undoing all our progress. This is a reality which is being experienced by all concerned inhabitants of the earth.

How can this be explained? The reason is clear: people do not possess a complete ideology, which favours peace, whereas the sole justification for violence is the force of public sentiment. When an activist feels the urge to become a world leader or when a community is provoked into avenging the losses it has suffered, no need of logical or rational justification is felt. The force of sentiment is sufficient to activate leaders and followers alike. But where adhering to peace or adopting a peaceful course of action is concerned this is possible only when there is a very strong justification for peace. While violence is instinctive, peace calls for strict mental discipline and self control to be exercised, everyone wants to assert himself by negating others, so that, one short emotional outburst is all that is needed for violence to be indulged in, unlike peaceful action, which requires serious thought to be given to it.

The only solution to this serious problem is for man to be in possession of a complete ideology of peace. The actual problem of today is that no ideology of peace in the real sense exists. Why is there this negative side to human psychology? It is directly related to the creation plan of the Creator. It acquires meaningfulness only in terms of God's plan of creation.

The present world has been designed by its Creator as a testing ground for mankind. Man has been granted full freedom of will in this world. But this freedom is not meant to produce anarchy. Its objective is to demonstrate whether man, despite having full freedom, can lead a disciplined life. He has to raise himself from the level of animal amorality to the level of human ethics. In spite of experiencing feelings of hatred and having the urge to be violent, he should become the embodiment of love and peace. When negative sentiments corrode his heart, he should be able to rid himself of them and make himself a positive thinker.

To put it briefly, despite possessing total freedom, he should of his own free will become an example of moral, disciplined behaviour. One who thus conducts himself will pass God's test. Only those who act in this way will be selected by the Lord, the Creator and Sustainer of this universe, as the beneficiaries of that most wonderful blessing—eternal paradise.

The study of psychology tells us that human beings are by nature egoists. Whenever their ego is hit, a hostile reaction is produced which easily becomes converted into hatred and the urge to do violence. This point has been dealt with very clearly by C.M. Joad in his book: "The Modern Wickedness." It is this psychological weakness in human beings due to which we find that differences often take the form of animosity, which frequently leads to violence.

This shows that violence is in no need of any ideology. Violence flares up, or can flare up on its own. But, so far as peace is concerned, it is a course that we adopt by choice. One has to make oneself intentionally peace-loving. That is, while violence occurs on its own, restoring a state of peace requires a positive and determined struggle.

Willingness to keep the peace—a matter of conscious decision-making—is a noble human quality. For peace, man has to curb his anger and be forgiving. He has to control his feelings of hatred and project feelings of love for others. If peace is to be maintained, negative thinking has to be suppressed and replaced with positive thinking. For peace to be a reality, he has to be a well-wisher rather than an ill-intentioned person.

For violence to erupt, provocation is enough, while for peace to prevail, man has to nullify provocation with moderation and restraint.

In the use of violence, man simply follows his basic instincts, while to promote peace, man has to give himself a complete moral overhaul. Only after such a conversion is the individual able to play the role of a peace-loving person.

The need is to convert non-peace into peace, for only after this conversion is he able to play the role of a peaceful person. That is why a comprehensive ideology of peace is necessary. Simply making appeals and pronouncements will not suffice for this purpose, for they will not persuade people to adopt peaceful ways.

This has been borne out by historical events and it is likewise my own personal experience. I have been engaged in a peace mission, for the last fifty years, and I can say with conviction that hundreds and thousands of youths who, spurred on by their emotions, had taken to violence or militancy, underwent a revolution in their thinking after listening to my reasoning and studying my writings which, by means of forceful arguments, established the paramouncy of peace. They abandoned the path of violence and opted for the path of peace.

I found that those youths, out of a lack of awareness, had mistakenly thought that violence was to be equated with bravery, and peaceful action with cowardice. They thought that there was everything to be gained by violence, but that peaceful methods would bring them nothing. This misapprehension caused them to think that violence meant advancement, and peace meant regression.

In other words they had an 'ideology' of violence, but no ideology of peace. Yet they became convinced by my arguments that there was no real ideology in favour of violence, and that positive ideology was only in favour of peace, in the real sense. Furthermore, the realization dawned on them that the violent course of action which they had taken in order to advance their own interests was ultimately suicidal, while the peaceful course of action which they had thought unproductive was, in fact, the true path to advancement.

After this intellectual discovery, their lives underwent a transformation. From being violent activists, they turned into peaceful activists. Indeed, in various parts of the world, there are a great number of youths who, after becoming fully aware of the truth of this matter, have abandoned violence in favour of engaging their energies in peaceful spheres of life—for instance, in education, social reform and the preaching of peace.

PEACE AND VIOLENCE

PEACE has been defined by scholars as the absence of war. Technically speaking, this definition is quite right. When there is no armed conflict in a society, a state of peace will automatically establish itself. The establishment of peace in a society is, however, not just a matter of putting an end to war and violence: that is only its initial phase. Whenever the state of peace prevails in a society in the real sense, its members will necessarily engage themselves in positive activities. Their energies will be channelised into the reconstruction of their own lives and of their social environment.

The establishment of peace in a society can be likened to removing a dam from a river. Human life, like a flowing river, wants to surge forward under its own momentum. When there is no obstruction, all life's activities will be set in motion, propelled by human nature itself. They come to a halt only when the artificial barriers of war and violence are placed before them. Peace, from the point of view of its result, is like an opening of all the doors of life to the fullest possible extent.

There are some who call this kind of peace negative. They say peace has no value unless it is accompanied by justice. If they are offered peace, pure and simple, they will not accept it. They hold that they should first be given justice and their rights, and then only can they live peacefully with others. "Peace with justice" is their watchword. This shows a lack of realism in their thinking. The truth is that justice does not directly follow on from a state of peace. The aim of establishing peace is, in fact, to open up opportunities for the achievement of justice, rather than the actual bringing of justice into being.

Peace, of course, is a highly desirable state of being because, once it is established, everyone has the opportunity to make plans, and then achieve whatever he wants. But those who insist on the prior condition of justice going hand in hand with peace will find neither peace nor justice. And they will continue to fight in the name of securing justice. In this way they will never let such peace prevail as will provide an atmosphere conducive to securing justice.

Peace is generally studied as the antithesis to war. But this is an extremely limited concept of peace. The truth is that peace relates to the entire spectrum of human life. In itself it is a complete ideology. Peace is the master key, which opens all doors to success. It paves the way for the success of sincere efforts in all spheres. In a state of peace, we can go about any task: without peace it is impossible to act constructively. This is true of all matters in life, both great and small.

The Difference between Peace and Violence

Peace is the result of planned action, while violence is purely an aggressive response to any kind of provocation. The peace-loving person first thinks and then acts. The violent person first acts and then thinks. There is hope in peaceful action from start to finish. In violent action, however, there are false hopes to begin with, which are soon followed by frustration.

The peace-loving person stands for truth, while the violent person stands for falsehood. The way of peace runs an even course from beginning to end, while the path of violence is strewn with obstacles. In peace, construction is all, while with violence, destruction is all. A peace-loving person lives with love in his heart for others, while a violent person is consumed with hatred for others. The peaceful course ends in success, while the violent course ends in frustration and regret.

In having recourse to peaceful methods, there is nothing to be lost and everything to be gained. Violent methods, on the contrary, bring no gains, only losses. The way of peace is the way of humanity, while the way of violence is the way of animality. While an act of peace is well within the ambit of the law, the act of violence is utterly lawless.

A peace-loving person ignores problems and avails of opportunities, while a violence-loving person leaves opportunities untapped and remains locked in a futile struggle with problems. While an act of peace causes the orchard of love and well-wishing to blossom, an act of

violence sows the seeds for a whole jungle of enmity and
hatred. The culture of peace is, in short, the culture of
goodness, while the culture of violence is the culture of
evil.

In peace, God's rights as well as human rights are
honoured. Where violence reigns, human rights as well
God's rights are violated. If peace is paradise, violence is
hell.

Where the opposite courses of peace and war are open
to man, peace is the true choice for him. War is only a
proof that he has made the wrong choice. That is a test in
which he has failed. The truth is that war and violence
are in no way valid options for any individual, community
or nation.

Although many allurements exist in this world, they
are there purely to put man to the test. They are not
something desirable for man. For instance, alcohol is
available, but it does not exist for man's consumption. It
is there rather for man to refrain from indulging in it and
thus prove his ability to distinguish between good and
bad. It is a temptation, in the avoidance of which he shows
that he is prudent and a man of principles. The same is
true of war. Although the way of war is open to all, the
noblest line of conduct is to refrain from opting for it.

The conditions prevailing in ancient times allowed for
war in self-defence. But this permission to go to war
conformed to the law of necessity. Now, in the present
situation, this need no longer exists, therefore there should
be a general ban on war.

The difference between the agricultural age and the industrial age

As regards war, all religions and all ethical systems are agreed upon one principle, and that is, that no matter how great the justification for waging war, i.e. even in an entirely lawful war, non-combatants must not be assailed or killed. The attacking of non-combatants is totally unacceptable.

Now let us look at how this principle is carried into effect in wartime. This kind of condition, i.e. the attacking only of combatants, could be fulfilled only in the agricultural age. Today, owing to scientific and technological developments, war is waged with explosive weapons which do widespread damage. When a bomb is dropped over an inhabited area, it cannot do otherwise than kill a large number of non-combatants along with the combatants. In reality, therefore, it is well-nigh impossible to meet this condition.

This shows that, in practice, man has only two options in present times: either he refrains from war on the grounds that the observance of humanitarian provisos is impracticable. Or else he commits the crime of hurling himself headlong into war, callously ignoring all humane considerations.

When we delve deeper into the matter, we discover another important truth. We now find that in present times, on the one hand, circumstances are such as do not allow us to meet all the desirable conditions of waging war, while, on the other hand, such resources have been made available by the industrial revolution as permit us to achieve our goals by purely peaceful means. Indeed, we may expect to win far greater victories today by peaceful means than could have been done in ancient times by waging war. It must be conceded that war, as fought in former ages, has been rendered a futile exercise by the modern industrial revolution.

When we keep this reality before us, we can safely conclude that violent war was the product of the circumstances prevailing in the agricultural age. In the industrial age, this kind of war, due to its counterproductive results, has been in principle rejected. With the end of the agricultural age, the way of violent struggle has at least theoretically come to an end. Now, in the present circumstances, the peaceful method is the only method. Now no excuse can justify violence or war.

The difference between peace and violence is aptly illustrated by the building of a bird's nest. A nest can be constructed only by a peaceful effort. Violence can only destroy it, not build it. The same is true of human life. If any constructive work is to be achieved in life, it must be through peaceful efforts. Violence can only destroy life. It cannot build it.

The Price of Peace

Everything has its price—even peace. No individual or group can have peace unless it is willing to pay for it in due measure. And that means showing willingness suffers losses.

According to the law that governs the system of the present world, on the principle of "no risk no gain", it is necessary for people to incur losses of different kinds. At times, they are unfairly challenged by others, they fall a prey to economic difficulties, they suffer losses of land and wealth, they meet with an accident or are deprived of certain benefits that should have been theirs by right, and so on. Unpleasant experiences of this kind, by the very law of nature, are undergone at one time or another in this world, by individuals, communities and nations. In such situations, if people are not willing to suffer any loss, the result will be violence. But if they are willing to make sacrifices, this will result in peace.

Opting for the way of patience and tolerance does not mean treading the path of defeat or retreat. It is, in fact, a future-oriented plan. It amounts to a voluntary acceptance of reality. This means that, even after losing something, one has always to remember that one is still in possession of many other things by utilizing which one can build anew.

The benefit of patience and tolerance is that, even after suffering losses, the bereft one does not lose his balance. In spite of temporary defeat, he never loses the ability to think cool-mindedly and, by making a realistic assessment of his situation, plans his life anew. By forgetting what is lost, he reorganizes his work on the basis of whatever he still possesses. Frustration yields pride of place to planning and he sets himself to starting his life's journey all over again.

One reliable feature of our world is that here the night is always followed by the morning. This world is full of possibilities and opportunities. Here, after losing one opportunity, man will find another. Here, if he finds one door closed to him, he will soon find many other doors open to him. In this way, there is always the possibility that, after the failure of one set of plans, he may work on another set and build his life afresh.

The truth is that in this world each piece of bad news is followed by good news. Each adverse incident gives man the good tidings that we should not fall a victim to frustration or lose heart. Rather we should muster enough courage to seek out new opportunities. Nature's system tells us in advance that our deprivation is not going to last forever. Soon we will be able to build a better world for ourselves. Soon our defeat will prove to be a victorious beginning.

Those who are unable to bear losses patiently tend to lapse into negative thinking. In this way, their life becomes a burden to themselves and to others. On the contrary, those who have patience and courage, build a new edifice on the ruins of the past. After the night comes the dawn, so that in its light they may continue their journey without a break. However, this noble end awaits only those who refrain from violence and engage themselves in peaceful activities, regardless of the circumstances.

Peace—A Great Power

The power of peace is far greater than the power of violence. One who, failing to recognize this truth, adopts a violent course of action in order to achieve his goals, demonstrates his own foolishness. For peace is the way of the wise, while violence is the way of the foolish.

Peace and war are not just two equal modes of achievement in the simple sense of the phrase. Rather they reflect two different standards of humanity. One who adopts the path of peace raises the level of humanity, while one who adopts the path of violence decidedly lowers it.

In moments of crisis, when the individual opts for the way of peace, he cultivates positive thinking. He raises his moral standards. He goes from strength to strength in the improvement of his own character. Indeed, he gives a practical proof of his being a human being. On the contrary, when a man opts for the path of violence to solve his problems, he slides down the slippery slope towards perdition. He makes it all too clear that he is suspect as a human being.

Inclinations towards peace or violence serve as indicators of the true character of the human being. If the former proves the humanity of the individual, the latter proves his animality, despite his appearing to be a human being.

Peaceable behaviour is indicative of self-control. Self-control is undoubtedly a very great strength: it saves man from engaging in negative activities like violence. One who does not have the power of self control will be enraged at times of provocation and will hurl himself into violent activities. Controlling one's anger is the way of the peaceful person, while losing one's self control when provoked is the way of the violent person.

Reconciliation is the best

In any controversy, one way to attempt to settle matters is for both parties to enter into violent confrontation. The better way to settle disputes is to effect a reconciliation at the very outset. Reconciliation is like a safety valve in any situation where there are conflicting interests and where tempers can become explosive. So at times of provocation, the best course to adopt is a conciliatory rather than a confrontational one. That is a law of nature.

However, it rarely happens that such reconciliation as can be effected exactly reflects the desires of both the parties. In the majority of cases, reconciliation is possible only on a unilateral basis. That is, one party has to suppress his own inclinations and show a willingness to put an end to the dispute in accordance with other party's wishes.

Why is this kind of unilateral reconciliation better? The main benefit is that without wasting one's energy and time in unnecessary wrangling, one is able to carry on a constructive course of action, whereas a state of confrontation puts a full stop to all such activity.

History shows that any success on the part of an individual or a community has been achieved by adopting the conciliatory method. The path of clash and confrontation has never led to any genuine success in this world. Reconciliation is vital, because it gives man the opportunity to utilize available opportunities to the fullest extent, whereas confrontation leads to his entire energies being channelized into planning the destruction of others. The work of construction, therefore, is never engaged in, although the secret of true success lies in construction and consolidation rather than in destroying supposed enemies.

Many people justify violence by saying that they have been the victims of plots and conspiracies and so must put an end to this by fighting. This excuse is quite baseless. What is generally regarded as a plot is, in actual fact, a manifestation of that plan of nature which has been established in the present world as a natural law.

In the present world, the actual problem for a community is not that it has enemies plotting against it. The actual problem is that it has failed to purge itself of the weaknesses that provide others with the opportunity to exploit it. An established state of peace is a safeguard against this kind of exploitation. Violence means rendering oneself insecure by breaking the defence line.

THE WAYS AND
MEANS OF PEACE

JUST as violence is a way of life, so is peace a complete culture in itself. Just as there are methods of violence, so are there clear principles and methods of peace. Here, we mention certain methods which are of relevance to the conduct of peaceful activities. This will show how the culture of peace can be established and how one's course of life can be planned, in all matters, so that all human beings may find the opportunities to realize their ambitions.

Tolerance is Peace

The result of intolerance is violence and the result of tolerance is peace. This sums up what peace and violence essentially are. An atmosphere of peace will prevail in any society which is characterized by tolerance, while an atmosphere of violence will prevail in any society in which the majority of the people are lacking in tolerance. And, according to the system of nature, violence is neither beneficial for its perpetrators, nor for those who have been subjected to violence.

Tolerance is a high moral and human quality, while intolerance is a descent to the animal level. The act of tolerance is not a matter of compulsion: it results naturally from the doer being of an elevated moral calibre. Any goal one strives to achieve by brute force, can always be better achieved by displaying tolerance. When an individual becomes intolerant in unpleasant situations, he considerably weakens himself and hence is unable to deal effectively with problems. But when he maintains an attitude of tolerance, he conserves all his energies, and is in a position to deal more effectively with the matters at hand.

Not descending to intolerant behaviour, in spite of facing unpleasant situations, is a clear proof of self-control. One who has this ability becomes so strengthened by it that no one can defeat him.

Avoidance, not confrontation

It is certainly possible to avoid violence, even although there may be reason to justify the option of violence. This is possible through the peaceful strategy of avoidance of conflict. Such avoidance is the most effective way of checking violence and is, indeed, the most important principle of a peaceful social life. Treading the path of avoidance keeps one within the peaceful sphere, while its very opposite, the way of confrontation, leads one into taking violent action against antagonists.

In the present world no individual or group is alone. There are many others with their own objectives, and they have their own separate agendas. For this reason, they often find themselves in confrontation with others.

In such a situation, there are two paths for man—avoidance or confrontation. There is no third option. Now, if man opts for the way of confrontation, the result will be a clash. It is evident from the entire history of humanity that an armed confrontation only intensifies feelings of animosity in people's hearts. It does not benefit either side in any real way. Therefore, the policy of avoidance should be favoured over that of confrontation. The way of avoidance not only saves one from further losses, but also allows one to continue on the path of progress without any hindrance. Indeed, any act of avoidance, appears to be benefitting the other party but its actual aim is to save one from the futility of confrontation, thus enabling the journey of one's life to continue without encountering any obstacle.

The approved method

A violent method is adopted only by those who have no patience or who do not believe in perseverance. Those who opt for a peaceful solution find that all the laws of nature come to their support. On the contrary, those who opt for violent methods can hope for no such backing. And those thus deprived cannot look forward to anything in this world of realities but failure and ruination.

What is meant by 'treading the path of peace'? It means that, even in the face of unpleasantness, no individual should lose his patience. In this way, his positive train of thought will not be upset and he may then clearly differentiate between the possible and the impossible.

Only then will he be able to set the possible as his goal. He should not expect immediate results. Rather, in going about his task, he should opt for the gradual way. He should not be depressed by his losses, but should rather engage himself in purposeful activities, with his eyes on the future. He should be content for the moment with what he receives at the moment and patiently wait for future blessings. He should keep his desires subservient to the laws of nature rather than try to keep the laws of nature subservient to his desires. The truth is that, patience is a totally positive attitude. It is neither negative nor passive.

A friend in the enemy

The way of violence only increases the enmity of opponents. On the contrary, the way of peace puts an end to such enmity. It even converts enmity into friendship. The study of human nature shows us that a potential friend could be there inside every enemy. We have to discover this friend, and accept as a miracle the fact that one who had at one time appeared to be our enemy became our closest friend.

The truth is that enmity is not something natural. It is an artificial reaction. Whenever for any reason anyone apparently becomes your enemy, you should remain mild-mannered in your dealings with him and try to behave well, even if you have to do so unilaterally and in the face of provocation. This peaceful response on your part will result in the subsiding of negative feelings in your enemy.

Your unilateral good behaviour will serve to awaken his dormant humanity, thus turning him into a new and better human being.

The truth is that the same temperament is common to every newborn child, which is why everyone is first Mr. Nature and only later on, becomes either Mr. Enemy or Mr. Friend. This means that the nature you possess is also possessed by your supposed enemy. Therefore, one must seek in an apparent enemy the common man in him, and each individual should expect from others what he expects for himself. The law of nature gives a guarantee that his expectations will not go unfulfilled.

The System of Cause and Effect

Violence is, to put it differently, laying the blame for one's own mistakes at the door of another. But this world is based on the principle of cause and effect, and when anyone suffers from some affliction, he should try to find the cause within himself, rather than attempt to find it elsewhere. As you sow, so shall you reap.

When this reality of life takes root in the mind of a human being, he will never hold anyone else responsible for his own afflictions, and take to violence against them. No, indeed, he will analyse his own actions objectively to discover his own shortcomings and rectify his mistakes in order that he may be saved from being the victim of unnecessary suffering.

Engaging in subversive activities against others, using one's own woes as a pretext, is like a patient holding his

neighbour responsible for his illness and starting a fight
with him. In a city where the traffic has to keep to the
right, anyone who thinks he can flout the rule of law by
driving his car on the left will certainly have an accident.

This accident would apparently have occurred due to
the collision of another's car with him, but he would have
no justification in saying that another motorist had injured
him by hitting his car. On the contrary, he should have to
admit that his car had collided with another, because he
had been driving on the wrong side of the street, while
the other motorist was on the right side.

The same is true of all other aspects of human
existence. Whenever you have to face any loss in life, you
must consider that whatever happened was due to your
own shortcomings. This is the way of peaceful thinking—
the correct way of thinking in the affairs of this life. If you
can think along the right lines, you will be able to set
yourself rectifying your mistakes, which will save your
future. If you take the opposite course, you will put all
the blame for your feelings of distress on others, and then,
by taking a violent option, you will destroy your future,
having already destroyed your past and present because
of choosing the same violent course.

Let the law of nature take its course

According to the law of nature in this world, truth lives
on, while falsehood is destined for obliteration. Given
this state of affairs, it is enough for the destruction of
falsehood that we observe a policy of silence. Speaking

out or holding protest movements to stir up agitation against falsehood is to give life to it, while adopting a policy of avoidance results in its dying a natural death.

Keeping quiet about falsehood means ignoring it, not giving any violent response to it, not launching any protests against it. However, opting for such a policy is possible only for those who are aware of the power of nature and who place their trust in it. Those who are unaware of it give life to falsehood by demonstrating against it.

Often people engage in violence in the name of obliterating falsehood. This is nothing but foolishness. Falsehood has no firm root. It is destined to vanish. In such a case, there is no need for unnecessary violence to obliterate it. The adoption of a peaceful course to counter falsehood is as good as extirpating it.

Anachronistic Policy

The present age is one of globalisation. The entire world has become a global village. Looked at from this viewpoint, violence or armed struggle in the present- day world has acquired the character of an anachronism. If you were to ask those engaged in armed confrontation why they had adopted this course, they would say that they had done so in order to overthrow the existing government. They would further say that they aimed at building a new system, and to attain their objective it was necessary to seize power. But all such thinking is the result of their being totally unaware of the spirit of the age.

The present age has undergone such a great transformation that the seizure of political power is no longer required. Even without possessing political power, those who aim at changing social systems can achieve anything that they want to through non-political institutions. Modern communications and industrialization have relegated government to a secondary position, signifying "administration" rather than monarchical or oligarchic rule. Now any task of reform or nation building can be done without aspiring to political eminence.

The truth is that political power has been reduced to little more than a headache for those who wield it. You should, therefore, leave this headache for others and set about peacefully realizing your goals. You will then see that you have won the war without going into battle. Without possessing political power, you have managed to receive all possible benefits, or perhaps even more than were formerly associated with political power.

Violence is the result of hatred

One of the chief reasons for violence is hatred. And hatred is mainly the result of negative thinking. Positive thinking and hatred do not go together. This being so, to maintain a peaceful society, it is essential that positive thinking should never be discouraged. Events should be explained in such a way that people do not lapse into negative thinking, but on the contrary, feel stimulated to think along positive lines.

The Politics of Religious Violence

Emotional politics is one reason for hatred and violence, especially when based on the slogan: 'Religion is in danger!' By presenting a wrong or exaggerated picture, certain writers and speakers try to give the impression that their religion is under threat from others. Now an emotional campaign is launched with great fervour in the name of safeguarding religion. Far from saving religion from danger, such politics only endangers society as a whole by destroying peace.

This concept of religion being at risk clearly implies that a community other than one's own is to blame. This fosters hatred in one group for another. And when a policy of confrontation fails to put an end to the supposed danger, frustration sets in. This leads to violence as a final strategy. And when violence does not give the desired result, suicide is resorted to. Youths, surcharged with emotion, resort to venting their ever-increasing hatred for their supposed enemy by carrying out suicide bombings. The politics of religion being "under attack" in its final phase turns into the politics of "religious" suicide. Launching their movements in the name of the revival of religion proves to be the death knell for themselves as well as for others. The truth is that the only way to extricate oneself from such destructive politics is to hold violence as a form of action to be rejected in all circumstances. No excuses, however weighty they may appear, should be treated as sufficient to justify the use of violence.

The present world is a world of differences. Every man is Mr. Different and every woman is Ms. Different. That is why all kinds of differences exist among people. But when these differences take on an emotional aspect, it leads people into malevolent conduct. And then society as a whole becomes wracked with violence.

There is only one possible solution to this problem. And that is to inculcate the notion that all members of society must work within a peaceful sphere, irrespective of general conditions. In no circumstances must they go outside the arena of peace. The correct mentality can be formed only when people are brought fully abreast of the fact that, in this world, any task can be performed through peace. No task can be performed successfully through violence. Violence contributes only to destruction—not to construction. A religion is never in danger. Any religion which appears to be in danger is no religion at all.

From revenge to violence

It often happens that if one person is hurt by another, or one group suffers at the hands of another, revenge is perceived as the immediate goal. Those who are bent on revenge tend to forget the warning of history—a warning inscribed on every wall in silent language: Think before seeking vengeance, that vengeance will be met with vengeance. In this way a chain of violence is built up, continues, and is brought to a conclusion only when both sides are so depleted in energy and resources that they are no longer able to exact vengeance.

Whenever an individual or a group has any cause for complaint, the solution lies not in retaliatory activities, but rather in continuing to move forward by adopting a policy of avoidance of conflict. Such avoidance puts an end to the problem at the very outset, while refusal to ignore the problem leads to an unending chain reaction of hatred, revenge and violence. Thus, the policy of avoidance of conflict is the way of the peace-loving ,while that of revenge is the way of the violent.

Revenge is always directed against another but, in actual fact, the greatest victim is the one who opts for this course. The heavy price to be paid for this revenge policy is that his mind becomes a storehouse of negative thinking. Instead of expending his resources on building his life, he begins to squander them on the destruction of others.

Say, an antagonist had caused him to use up fifty percent of his energies, resources, etc., he would himself, as a result of his policy of revenge, fritter away the other 50%.

Taken to logical extremes, revenge would imply that after an attempt on one's life, one would launch out on a course which would end in one's own death! The truth is that revenge is an evil, whatever the circumstances, while refraining from revenge by ignoring the matter at issue is at all events a virtue. If the taker of revenge is your enemy, after returning revenge for revenge, you become your own enemy. And those who turn their own enemy cannot be saved from destruction by anyone.

Formula for Social Peace

Peace is nature. In any society, peace is disturbed only when any violent activity causes man to deviate from his nature. The truth is that every one of us has his ego. It is a state of mind which, if provoked, takes no time in flaring up and wreaking havoc. But by nature, in accordance with the system of creation, it generally lies dormant. The easiest way, therefore, to have a peaceful society is to let this ego remain undisturbed. Social peace is disturbed by those whose egos have been provoked. If we refrain from such provocation, there will be no disturbance of the social peace. This shows that the establishment and maintenance of social peace are within our control, and are not at the mercy of anti-social elements. This shows that if you do not provoke the ego of others, you will certainly remain safe from their violence.

The possession of weapons is no guarantee of social security. The principle of social security is to become a peace-loving neighbour for others. Perpetrate no violence upon others and you will, of necessity, be safe from the evil and violence of others. If you hate others you will receive hate from them in return. If you have feelings of love and well-wishing for them, you will receive the same from them. In this world, peace is received in return for peace and violence is received in return for violence.

Terrorism—a barbaric course

The evil of terrorism has come to be a present-day affliction. It is widely condemned, but what terrorism is has not yet been clearly defined. After a great deal of thought on this subject, I have come to the conclusion that terrorism is definable as armed action carried out by non-governmental organizations. Certainly, the public have the right to peacefully present their point of view, but on no consideration do they have the right to engage in militancy, for armed movements of this sort run counter to accepted national and international principles. What is known as terrorism in present times is the result of armed action by NGO'S.

Moreover, war can be waged only by an established government. And even for an established government there are a number of essential conditions for launching armed campaigns. For instance, it can only fight a defensive battle. It cannot commit aggression. Similarly, even a lawful war can be fought only after making a formal declaration of war. There is no room for undeclared war in civilized society. Then, even in a lawful defensive battle, a government must issue strict orders that only combatants may be attacked. Killing or injuring non-combatants is not lawful even in a state of war.

According to established humanitarian principles, only one form of war is acceptable and that is one waged unavoidably in self-defence. Any other kind of war, for instance, aggressive war, proxy war, guerrilla war, undeclared war –are all totally unlawful according to international ethics. On no consideration can these wars be held lawful.

According to the above definition, any movement based on terrorism is certainly unlawful. It cannot be justified simply by giving it a high-sounding name. Any attempt to achieve human objectives by engaging in terrorism, rather than using lawful means to do so, is to transgress all bounds.

Modern terrorism must, therefore, be brought to an end. But this cannot be done through counter attacks. For one thing, this would be like trying to quell non-state terrorism by state terrorism. And for another, modern terrorism derives its strength less form guns and bombs than from its ideology. That is why a counter ideology rather than counter-bombing would the more effectively put an end to terrorism.

The terrorists' self-styled ideology gives them the conviction that, by dying in battle, they become martyrs and that, as such, they will have a new and far better life in paradise. It is this belief, which has made suicide bombing totally acceptable to them. Given this situation, it is only when their self-styled ideology is shown to be baseless by producing a counter ideology that their violent actions will ever come to an end.

It should be appreciated, moreover, that the present terrorists, many of them very young people, would never be able to continue their efforts without the vast monetary contributions, public sympathy and adulation as heroes, which as "active militants" they receive from "passive" militants, that is to say, from those who are not actively engaged in violent activities.

The passive militants are, so to speak, the second line of terrorism. Their role is an important one, that of providing infrastructure and logistic support. A war can be successfully waged only if the supply lines continue to provide all military requirements without any disruption. If they were to be cut off, war would automatically come to an end, just as a man would die if his oxygen supply were stopped. But, ideologically, passive militants regard it as their duty to give full assistance to active terrorists. And if such terrorists are in their thousands, the number of their supporters runs into millions. This being so, the annihilation of known active terrorists would not suffice to put an end to the phenomenon of terrorism.

It is essential, therefore, that the issue of the enormous support given by the world-wide network of passive terrorists be immediately addressed. Their minds must be changed. Their violent thinking must be transformed into pacifism. Only then will it be possible to rid the world of the menace of terrorism.

POSITIVE STATUS
QUOISM

PEACEFUL method in one respect, is another name for status quoism. The status quoism of a peace-loving person is not a form of inaction, it is rather a positive plan of action, in the real sense of the word. That is, the peace-love accepts the status quo to remove himself from the point of confrontation to other fields where he may proceed with constructive action. Instead of becoming embroiled in problems he looks to the future aid directs his energies towards the availing of opportunities. That is why the status quoism of a peace-loving person is indeed positive status quoism.

In this world of diverse interests, positive status quoism is the optimal base for the conception and implementation of constructive projects. Taking up this position may call for special virtues such as insightfulness as well as the capacity for the most superior type of planning. Thus it brings twofold benefit. Firstly, no disturbance of the peace, and secondly and ultimately, the guarantee of success. This formula can thus be summed up: Avoid confrontation, adopt peaceful activism.

Flowers and their Thorns

In our world there are flowers, but there are also thorns. It is therefore a common experience for one who wants to engage in any positive activity to feel that there are obstacles in his way, perhaps by the very law of nature. This applies to the individual as well as to the entire nation. Now one way of addressing such a situation is for him to set about removing all obstacles from the path and only then beginning to work towards his goal. This method is generally defined as radicalism.

Radicalism greatly appeals to extremists or to those who are guided by their emotions. But it is impractical in so far as achieving any positive goal is concerned. While radicalism may be effectively used for the purposes of destruction, it is worse than useless when it comes to construction. Once the path of radicalism has been chosen, not only does the prevalent system fall apart, but in the process of what are essentially ruinous activities, all those social traditions which had taken centuries to build, simply fall to pieces. Then as a result of bloodshed and violent confrontation, innumerable people fall victim to all kinds of afflictions. While experience shows that the method of radicalism is ideologically very attractive, in terms of its practical outcome, it is devoid of all merit.

Another method is that of avoiding confrontation with the status quo and chalking out a plan for possible action within possible spheres. By temporarily accepting the status quo, current opportunities may then be availed of.

This is the positive status quoism to which I referred at the beginning of this chapter.

The method of radicalism invariably produces violence: on the contrary, positive status quoism fulfills its target by keeping the peace in society. While the former invariably aggravates the problem, the latter, by avoiding friction, proceeds smoothly, without creating any problems. If one is the way to perversion, the other is the way to construction.

A De-linking Policy

Positive status quoism can also be defined as a de-linking policy, which entails finding ways of peaceful action despite the existence of controversies. This means that irrespective of there being a confrontational state of affairs or other adverse circumstances. Such strategies should be adopted as may prevent war being waged and violence taking place. Controversial issues must be set aside so that present opportunities may be availed of in an atmosphere of peace. In following this policy, two gains simultaneously accrue: one, the establishment of peace, notwithstanding the pernicious atmosphere created by controversies; and, two, the optimization of work opportunities, despite the presence of problems. One great benefit of this de-linking policy—in that it is the most felicitous natural formula for the establishment of peace— is that conducive circumstances for result-oriented actions are no longer a matter of the past, but become an actuality today.

Aspects of Positive Thinking

Positive status quoism is undoubtedly the most successful strategy for the construction of a peaceful life. The essential condition for the utilization of this strategy, however, is for man to develop the kind of positive attitude which will enable him to rise above his circumstances. Even in the most adverse situations, he should be able to weather all storms as do the big birds of the storm. His thinking should not be the result of prior conditioning. He should rather think out and plan his actions without any prejudice.

One of the obstacles to adopting positive status quoism is the tendency to give way to anger and vengefulness. Such an attitude so poisons man's mind that he is no longer able to think objectively. It is this lack of objectivity which is the main reason for failing to adopt a positive stance.

Anger is a weakness

Anger is the killer of peace. Anger often results in violence. Giving vent to anger is a sign of weakness, whereas the mastering of anger is a sign of power. Anger, moreover, confounds one's thinking capacity. The angry man can neither understand any issue in a clear-headed way, nor can he give a response which is adequate to the situation. What is worse is that when an individual is angry, he is all too prone to turn to violence. But the truth is that violence is no solution to any problem. For one who can prevent himself from succumbing to anger, there is no situation which he will not be able to turn to good account. He will seek a peaceful solution—the only sure way to solve any problem.

Man's mind has extraordinary potential. When he is not angry, he is in a position to utilize his capabilities to the best advantage. But when he is angry, his mental balance is lost. He is not in a position to make the full use of such mental capabilities as would be to his own benefit. In short, not becoming angry is victory, while becoming angry is defeat.

It should be borne in mind also, that overcoming anger is not simply a matter of suppressing one's emotions. It means being able to deal with the problem by rising above the negativism of anger. One should be able to respond, uninfluenced by emotion in spite of being provoked. This principle applies not only to the individual but also to entire nations. Positive status quoism is undoubtedly the surest way to success, but only those can adopt this method who have the ability to think independently of the psychology of anger.

The principle of positive status quoism can be adopted only by those who have the mental discipline not to resort to violence, despite facing unpleasant situations. Those who cannot curb violent tendencies will never be able to experience the benefits of positive status quoism.

The Way of Non-Violence

One of the laws of nature is that non-violence is result-oriented, while violence is destruction-oriented. Therefore, if the individual confines his activities to the field of gentleness and non-violence, his work will yield results, whereas one who opts for the way of violence and intolerance regresses instead of advancing.

The truth is that whenever anyone opts for the way of intolerance and violence, his energies are unnecessarily divided between two fronts—internal construction and doing battle with the external foe, whereas one who opts for gentleness and non-violence can devote all his available energy and resources to the one front of internal consolidation alone, and as a natural result, he can achieve a far greater success.

This is the law of nature which is operative in our world. Here if one is to achieve any estimable goal, it will only be by adhering to this system of nature which is entirely based on the principle of peace and non-violence. Therefore, here one can be successful by adhering to, and not by deviating from this law. Non-violent activism can in fact, be equated with positive status quoism.

The Benefits of Peace

It is a fact that all worthy feats in this world have been performed by peaceful endeavour. No great or noble task has ever been carried out by the power of violence. This applies equally to scientific discoveries and technological progress. Neither educational institutions nor research institutes have ever been established by violent means. Iron's conversion into machines and major city planning have all been done by the power of peace, not of violence. Right from ensuring social welfare to the setting up of the relevant infrastructure—all progressive measures have been carried into effect by peaceful strategies.

Violence per se is destructive and no constructive result can ever come from a destructive act. This is the law of nature and as such is immutable.

The Solution to the Problem of Enmity

People generally hold that so and so community or nation is their enemy. Then, for most people, enmity becomes both the cause of and justification for taking to a course of violence. They take up an aggressive stance, openly or covertly, ostensibly to put an end to the enmity. But this is as misconceived a plan of action as any could be which has been devised on the supposition that war can be any kind of solution.

They fail to realize that the best solution to the problem of enmity lies in the way of positive status quoism, which facilitates dealing peacefully with the enemy. This is possible because positive status quoism is a psychological condition which enables us to deal with the enemy in such a cool-minded way that all animus will of itself disappear once and for all.

It is imperative that we regard enemies as superficial rather than as integral parts of our existence, and we should recognize that the hostility of any foe can be brought to an end by positive strategy. The enemy can be likened to the dust sticking to glass. Such dust can easily be washed off with water. The real problem will arise only when we have no water (i.e. a positive strategy) to wash off the dust.

It takes two hands to clap. One hand on its own cannot clap. Similarly, enmity is a two-sided matter. If someone turns your enemy, you should not respond to this with hostility. Not returning enmity for enmity is the most successful solution to the problem. Adopting positive behaviour towards the enemy can yield such beneficial results that your former enemy could one day turn out to be your friend.

Violence is the result of frustration

One advantage of positive status quoism is that it obviates the baneful effects of frustration that come from a sense of deprivation. Bright prospects are discernible in all situations, however unfavourable those situations might appear. The miraculous benefit of positive status quoism is that it gives human beings unlimited courage. It saves them in all situations from becoming so discouraged that all doors appear closed, and they fail to identify any viable course of action.

Violence results from a feeling of deprivation, while peace results from a sense of discovery. Those who have the notion that they have been deprived of what is rightfully theirs suffer perennially from negative psychology. It is this negativism that frequently takes the form of violence. But those who live with the positive feeling that they have experienced the feeling of discovery enjoy mental peace. Their lives remain eternally peaceful.

Those individuals or groups who feel hatred for others, and who stoop to violence in their dealings with them, prove by their behaviour that their grievances derive from a sense of deprivation. On the contrary, those individuals or groups who lead peaceful lives prove by their behaviour that they have experienced the feeling of finding what they truly desire in life. The mind of a frustrated person is always obsessed with the prevalent state of affairs. While a person whose mind is free from the psychology of frustration will be capable of thinking by rising above the immediate circumstances. Thus a frustrated person is a present–oriented person while a person free from frustration is a future oriented person.

Violence Unnecessary

Social violence is against real human nature. Violence, the greatest of all crimes, is lethal to humanity. In spite of this, why do people engage in violence? The reason is that they take into account only present conditions, and lack the ability to see future prospects. Then such people find self-styled justifications for engaging in violence. Their version of justification appears to them to be based on logical argument, but in actual fact their arguments are fallacious. In defiance of all rational opinion, they adhere to the notion that, in their own case, for such and such reason, engaging in violence has become morally justified.

But the truth is that any so-called justification for violence is invalid. Whenever an individual or a group engages in violence, they have at one and the same time the option of a non-violent or peaceful method. This being so, why should violence be resorted to at all? When the opportunity to achieve one's objective is available without having recourse to violence, why should everyone opt for violent methods? The truth is that violence must be in principle discarded absolutely and peace must be adopted absolutely. Therefore, man ought not to engage in violence on any pretext. He must adhere to a peaceful course of action in all situations.

Patience is the Secret of Success

One element of positive status-quoism is the "wait and see" policy. This means that whatever man is easily able to do at the present time should be done, while whatever he feels presents too many difficulties should be postponed until the situation seems more favourable.

It often happens that whenever one is faced with difficult situations or one undergoes some bitter experience, out of sheer exasperation, one resorts to violence. But this kind of reaction is a result of deviation from nature. The truth is that the law of nature always favours those who adopt a realistic path. If such individuals or groups who stand by truth and justice do not act in an over-hasty manner and remain patient, such favourable conditions are ultimately produced for them that success will come to them on its own.

In the most cases, failure awaits those who are so impatient that they act emotionally, without giving much thought to the repercussions. On the contrary, those who opt for the way of patience are destined to be successful.

When an individual adopts the path of patience, he is following the path of nature. And when he adopts the path of impatience, he deviates from the path of nature. And one who strays from the path of nature has no prospects of success in this world of God.

Future-Oriented policy

To put it another way, positive status-quoism can also be thought of as a form of foresight. As a policy, it is in accordance with the natural law of "wait and see". There are times when each individual and community find themselves in the kind of situations in which they begin to feel that they are faced with certain obstacles, which prevent their making any headway. In such cases, most people come—consciously or unconsciously—to regard such difficult circumstances as a permanent condition. And as such they begin to wrestle with the circumstances in order to remove the hurdles. Fighting of this kind always proves futile. It only results in making things go from bad to worse. It should be remembered that difficult circumstances are never here to stay. They are always of an ephemeral nature. This being so, the easy solution to this problem is to ignore it, rather than unnecessarily wage

war on the circumstances. This policy will preserve man's
mental peace, and whatever lies in store for him will in
time become available to him.

Whenever man is confronted with any problem, he
wants it to be solved without delay. This is where he
actually goes wrong. If he could just shelve his problems
at least for a short time, he would find that solutions
would present themselves which had nothing to do with
combating circumstances head on, or with coming into
confrontation with opponents.

None of his problems would remain such for an
indefinite period of time. In most cases violence takes
place only because this principle, not being generally
understood, is not applied in daily living.

Avoidance of controversy

Positive status-quoism is undoubtedly a certain guarantee
of success. But adherence to the method of status-quoism
is possible only for one who has the ability to refrain from
the policy of confrontation, in spite of provocation, and
who never on any pretext engages in retaliation.

Proceeding by avoidance of confrontation is the secret
of success. Avoidance of controversy means not giving
any opportunity to others to create friction. That is,
whenever differences arise between one party and another,
their settlement should be confined to a peaceful sphere
of negotiation. It should never happen that differences
escalate into actual confrontation between two parties.

In the present world it often happens that, on some

point or the other, tension arises between two parties. This tension is in itself something natural. There is no escape from it, whatever the situation may be. What is really worthy of consideration is that this difference should not be allowed to escalate indefinitely.

What does it mean for differences to remain within limits? It means that differences must be confined to the peaceful sphere. When differences reach the actual stage of clash and violence, then all limits have been crossed. There is nothing wrong in differences being confined within limits: what is wrong is for differences to cross all normal bounds of decency.

For one who wants to pursue some serious goal successfully, it is necessary that only those points come under discussion which are related to this objective. The discussion of anything other than the actual goal is anathema to a man with a mission.

But how may a non-confrontational atmosphere between the speaker and the addressee be established? The answer is that this atmosphere can be produced only unilaterally by a display of patience on the part of the one who has the positive goal before him. From the practical point of view, no other way is possible. A purposeful man, by his avoidance of friction, has to maintain a normal atmosphere between himself and possible antagonists, so that his onward journey may proceed unhampered. It is such wisdom as provides a sound basis for positive status quoism.

GOING AGAINST THE CREATION PLAN

SUBSCRIBING to the notion that violence is a viable method of gaining one's ends and then launching oneself on a violent course of action are against the creation plan of nature. Neither the concept nor the deeds stemming therefrom are in accord with the divine scheme of things. That is why the violent way is destined to produce no good results and serves no end save that of destruction.

If a farmer has a fertile piece of land, he can grow crops in abundance. But this will be possible only if he follows an appropriate method which is in consonance with nature. If, however, he mindlessly starts pelting his fields with stones or dropping bombs on them, he will never be able to harvest the desired crops. In spite of being the owner of fertile acres, he will be no better off than one who has not a square yard of land to his name. The same is true of human life. Human life flourishes in an atmosphere of peace, but is destroyed in an atmosphere of violence.

Violence is the outcome of differences between people. One who believes in violent methods considers differences as evil or an obstacle in his path. For this reason, he becomes bent on obliterating evil, for he thinks that he can achieve his objective only when he has removed the differences between himself and others. This is a great misunderstanding, for differences are not man-made. They are ordained by the Creator Himself, and are an essential part of nature. And something which is an essential part of nature cannot be brought to an end. We can only accept nature. Eliminating it is beyond our power. That is why when one group is annihilated in the name of differences, another such group immediately takes its place, and so it goes on and on quite endlessly. That is why this chain of action and reaction over the issue of differences can never be halted.

The method of violence goes against the plan of nature, which ensures that each individual has full opportunities to perform his or her role in human progress by exploiting his or her capabilities to the fullest extent. This benefit can be availed of only in a peaceful atmosphere. The perpetrators of violence, by categorizing people as enemies, attempt to obliterate the precious lives of human beings, even before they have had the opportunity to utilize their potential and benefit humanity.

According to the law of nature, any great task always requires the support of society as a whole. Without collective participation, no one can accomplish great feats. And this can materialize only in a peaceful atmosphere. Mutual co-operation is just not possible in an atmosphere of violence. In such an atmosphere people tend to be psychologically unbalanced. How then can mutual co-operation become possible in such an environment?

One of the evils of violence is that, in the vicious atmosphere created by it, there is no possibility of any sustainable development. Any great task of progress becomes result-oriented only after long-term planning and action. This kind of planning can make headway only in a peaceful atmosphere. In a violent atmosphere such plans face setbacks time and time again, without any progress being made: on the pretext of killing the enemy, the process of human progress is dealt a death blow.

The worst ill effect of the use of violence is that one receives nothing in return, and perhaps even forfeits previous gains. Any victory earned by means of violence is actually a defeat.

What is violence? It is a wrong choice made by one suffering from the feeling of deprivation. Any group, rightly or wrongly, may suffer from this feeling. There is only one useful way of getting rid of it and that is by peaceful means. The violent method is so lethal that it is no choice at all for anybody. Violence, from the point of view of its result, only adds to this feeling of deprivation, instead of putting an end to it. Violence is nothing but an outburst of a provoked person. Violence provides no positive solution to any problem.

Victory is also a defeat

King Pyrrhus, a Greek king of the third century BC, went to war with the Romans. Ultimately, he won a complete, but costly victory over the Roman army. In this prolonged battle his armies were destroyed, and his country's economy was totally devastated. For King Pyrrhus it was apparently a victory, but its result was nothing more or less than a defeat. It was his costly military successes which gave rise to the now current phrase "pyrrhic victory".

When we look into the history of different wars, it would be no exaggeration to say that most victories are pyrrhic in nature. Each victor has to suffer two losses. Firstly, he sacrifices life, wealth and resources, and secondly, he loses the love and respect of the vanquished. No victor can avoid suffering these losses. The only difference between one victor and another is that while some victors suffer their losses sooner, others suffer them later.

This matter of loss relates only to the violent method. A peaceful method leads to a totally different outcome. Once the peaceful method has been employed, victory and victory alone ensues: there is no room for defeat. Even if a peaceful method does apparently lead to a defeat, the final outcome is even then a victory. For, by using a peaceful method, one might lose a war, but one does not lose opportunities. One still has opportunities and possibilities, by availing of which one can start one's life all over again and reach the destination of success.

The age of war has come to an end

In ancient and mediaeval times, military encounters took place in the form of hand-to-hand fighting between soldiers wielding swords. But in modern times, highly sophisticated weapons such as nuclear missiles are used.

The basic difference between early and modern warfare is in the extent of the carnage in each case. The wielding of swords could sever the heads of only a few of the combatants, but now in the atomic age the equation has totally changed. For now war means general destruction. Moreover, the bomb aimed at the enemy is destructive to the user too. When we face up to these hard facts, we have to concede that war has become a futile exercise. War is now only a manifestation of madness, instead of being a measure calculated to enable one to achieve one's objective. After the emergence of nuclear weapons, war has become a thing to be abhorred and abandoned. When we can see that resorting to war shows no positive results, then waging it, far from being a wise step, is nothing short of madness.

It is believed by some that the establishment of peace requires a world government. This would require an armed police force and an army, on the strength of which peace would be established all over the world. But this concept of world government is impracticable, for it would only serve the purpose in a very limited way. The scheme of world government for establishing peace is far from ideal.

Let us suppose that such a world government were to come into being. It would be able to establish peace only at the level of administration. In other words, this projected world government could at best establish social peace. But what is more important than this is mental peace, which cannot be brought about by any world government.

Peace in the form of social stability, as enforced by established governments, was prevalent in the monarchies of ancient times. But the desired results could never be achieved. The Roman Empire provides one such example. During its rule which lasted for more than a thousand years, it established peace over a large area of the globe. This was known as the Pax Romana. But in spite of the establishment of peace for such a long period of time, no scientific or intellectual progress could be made.

This shows that, in spite of the desirability of social peace, it would only be partially useful for human progress. The real process of human progress is set in motion only when the individuals making up society have the capability for peaceful thinking.

Along with peace as an external manifestation, it is essential for human progress that people have internal peace, so that they do not live lives full of unnecessary tension, stress and contradictions. The most essential condition for human progress is that the thinking process, once set in motion, should not in encountering obstacles, become perverted. This is essential to the development of one's personality. Only by this process can the individual attain to the highest spiritual and intellectual level.

Peace is undoubtedly an essential condition for human progress. It is, indeed, the basis of all human progress. If social and political peace accounts for 50% of this basis, then mental and spiritual peace accounts for the other 50%. The establishment of peace on national and international fronts appears, in practice, to be difficult.

Perhaps, in the ideal sense, it is not attainable at all. But in all situations, peace of mind can certainly be attained. So far as external peace is concerned, it is necessary for everyone to cooperate in order to maintain it. But to achieve inner peace of mind, little or no external cooperation is required. An individual, by his or her own personal decision, can attain such peace, even when all others have turned inimical to the idea. This advantage possessed by the individual is undoubtedly the most fortunate thing. Indeed, there is no blessing greater than this.

A MANIFESTO
OF PEACE

PEACE is the only religion for both man and the universe. In a peaceful environment all good things are possible, whereas in the absence of peace, we cannot achieve anything of a positive nature, either as individuals, or as a community. The same holds true at national and international levels.

What is Peace?

Scholars have defined peace thus: "Peace is the absence of war." This definition is absolutely correct. Peace in fact means the absence of a situation of war or violence.

However, some people hold this definition of peace to be inadequate. They say that peace should be accompanied by justice; that peace devoid of justice is no peace. But setting such a condition for the attainment of peace is impractical. This is because peace on its own does not bring justice. That is, justice is not necessarily an element of peace. What peace does, in actual fact, is to open up opportunities. It creates favourable conditions that would enable us to strive for justice and other constructive ends. Peace is always desirable for its own sake. Everything else comes after peace, not along with peace.

A peace policy always serves as a peace 'bomb', in the sense that it conquers the enemy without any bloodshed. History shows that the peace bomb has always proved to be mightier than the violence bomb.

A peace 'bomb' means life, and a violent bomb means death. A peace 'bomb' leads to construction, while a violent bomb leads to destruction. Likewise, a peace 'bomb' brings progress, while a violent bomb brings annihilation. Peace enhances creativity, whereas violence does the very opposite. The power of a peace 'bomb' is based on love, while that of a violent bomb is based on hatred.

We find a very interesting example of a peaceful method in India. India's freedom struggle was started in 1857. But, even after more than 60 years of sacrifice, the desired political goal remained a distant dream. Then, in 1920, Gandhi emerged as the leader of the freedom struggle. Taking a U-turn, he abandoned the violent method and opted for a peaceful course of action for the freedom movement.

Things took a miraculous turn after that, with the British Empire becoming paralysed: a non-violent Gandhi had taken away from the British any justification for the use of violence. The following anecdote is an apt illustration. When Gandhi launched his freedom movement in India by following a peaceful method instead of resorting to violent means, a British officer sent a telegram to his secretariat in these words:

"Kindly wire instructions how to kill a tiger non-violently."

Therefore the success which was not forthcoming, even after a long and violent struggle, was achieved by peaceful method in a short period of time.

Peace—A Complete Code of Conduct

Violence and peace both have wide connotations. Violence includes everything from hatred to war. The same is true of peace, which includes everything from tolerance to love. Both violence and peace are the results of human thinking. Those who engage in violent activities are the worst people in this world, while those who opt for peaceful behaviour are the best. Peace means normalcy, and normalcy provides all such opportunities as favour the growth of a healthy environment. A natural condition should prevail, where people can live and work without any external hindrance.

Violence closes the doors to positive activities, while peace opens the doors to them. It creates an atmosphere of positive living for the individual, society and the nation at large. All kinds of achievements are possible in an environment of peace. If violent situations hamper opportunities, peace helps favourable situations to flourish, where man's creative abilities can be nurtured and developed.

While peace is a boon for human society, violence is a curse. Peace is an asset, and violence is a liability. Peace is love and violence is hatred. Peace is amity and violence is enmity. Peace brings people closer and violence distances them. Peace fosters a high level of human culture and helps it to flourish, whereas violence breeds a jungle culture. Peace elevates humanity to the level of civilized social existence, whereas violence causes a descent into barbarism. Peace promotes life, while violence is the harbinger of death and destruction. Peace brings the good elements of a society into prominence, while violence does the very opposite.

Peace Turns Minus into Plus

According to a German psychologist, Alfred Adler, a unique quality possessed by human beings is 'their power to turn a minus into a plus'. What enables man to perform this extraordinary feat? The only answer is that it is through peace. The human brain is a treasure house of unlimited power. If man loses his peace of mind at a time of crisis, he is not in a position to utilize his mental capacity in a positive way. Negative thinking is an obstacle to human development, while positive thinking is like a life-giver in that it stimulates human capacities. Therefore, when an individual or a nation is able to maintain peace in every situation, infinite possibilities open up. This is when minus can be turned into plus.

The Way to Attain Peace

Peace is essential for a better way of living—peace of mind, peace in the family and peace in nature. Today, in our modern, technological world, man apparently has access to everything he desires. In the absence of peace, however, everything has been rendered meaningless. What is needed to redress the balance is love, compassion, tolerance, forbearance and the spirit of co-existence.

How can we attain peace? The formula is very simple. Take your share without usurping that of others. Fulfill your needs without depriving others of theirs. Satisfy your desires without thwarting others and fulfil your ambitions without denying others the right to do likewise. In short, solve your own problems without creating problems for your fellow creatures. Peaceful co-existence is the only way of existence in this world.

However, a peaceful life can be achieved only when human beings learn what their limitations ought to be. According to the Divine law, you can take from the world whatever will satisfy your need—not your greed. You may do business with others, but you may not exploit them. You may also establish your individuality, but not at the cost of the family and society. In daily existence, you may lead your life by maintaining social traditions and not by destroying them. You have the freedom to lead your own life, but by caring in the process for the rest of your society and not by neglecting it. Resources may be utilized for the benefit of humanity, but not for the sake of destruction. You are free to use peaceful methods, but you are not entitled to use violence. You can make use of nature, but only by maintaining its balance: the equilibrium of nature must never be disturbed. You have the freedom to use nuclear energy for peaceful purposes, but not to manufacture destructive weapons. You are at liberty to nurture feelings of love and compassion, but not to give way to hatred and prejudice. You are free to fulfil your physical desires, but not by spiritually killing your soul. In short, you have the freedom to enjoy life by sharing with others, but certainly not by eliminating them.

The Price of Peace

We cannot have anything in this world without paying for it. Everything has its price and this is particularly true of peace. If we want peace, we should be ready to pay for it or stand deprived of it. What is the price of peace? It is simply tolerance. We live in a world of differences, and these differences cannot be eliminated. Therefore, we have only two options before us: adopting the policy of either tolerance or intolerance. While the latter leads to violence, the former ensures peace. Where there is tolerance there is peace, and where there is intolerance, there is war and violence. This is the only universal formula of tolerance for peace, and this same formula may be successfully applied to one's family life and to social life, as well as at the international level. Peace requires us to foster a culture of tolerance, for intolerance can lead only to war.

Nature—A Model of Peace

In the present world the root cause of most of our problems is traceable to our deviation from the peaceful model of nature—the best model for us to follow. All the dilemmas we are facing today arise because we have not followed nature's lead.

The stars and planets are in continual motion in their orbits, but they never collide with one another. This serves to show man how to proceed to his destination in life without coming into conflict with others. The sun too is an excellent model. It shows us how we should give life to others in a totally undiscriminating way. The tree is also a shining example to man, in supplying healthy and beneficial oxygen in exchange for harmful gas, that is, carbon dioxide. And just look at how the flowers spread fragrance all around, regardless of whether they are appreciated for it or not. A flowing stream is likewise a model when it irrigates the fields without expecting anything in return. Without the inculcation of these altruistic values among human beings, no meaningful life on earth is possible.

In short, positivity prevails throughout Nature. Negativity just does not exist in the natural world. This teaches us the lesson that we should give a positive response at all times, even in negative situations.

The Beautiful World of Nature

In this world, positive living is not of relevance solely to moral behaviour. Rather, it is incumbent upon us to follow a positive course at all times and in all situations. For, in this vast universe, there is only our tiny earth on which human beings may survive. To date, there is no other spot in the cosmos where we have discovered life-supporting systems. Preserving Nature, therefore, is synonymous with sustaining life, while destroying Nature will lead to total extinction. In short, consistently engaging in positive living amounts to saving life, while failing to do so is a certain way of committing suicide.

This beautiful world of nature created by God is well on its way to being ruined by man. Widespread violence, ecological disturbance and global warming have together become a menace greater than that of a third world war. Indeed, it is as if a third world war has already been thrust upon us. This is the biggest threat we are facing today. We have to work unitedly and sincerely to save Nature in the interest of all of humanity.

Nuclear Arms for What?

Nuclear bombs and other destructive devices are totally against the divine scheme prevailing in the beautiful world of nature. Why then should there be the present stockpiling of nuclear arms, which is the greatest threat not only to peace but also to the very survival of mankind?

Here it should be stressed, that nuclear arms are not usable. A weapon of mass destruction, like an atom bomb, can be used only once. So, Hiroshima Nagasaki represented a full stop— not a comma. Then why are some countries acquiring more and more nuclear bombs? The answer is that they want to maintain their status as nuclear powers. There is, however, an alternative far superior to their possessing the status of a nuclear power. That is, they must destroy all nuclear bombs. Such an action would lead to a peace 'explosion'. Anyone who dared to do so, would emerge as a spiritual winner, and a moral superpower, unlike the competitors in the nuclear race, where there can be no winner.

It is a fact that being a moral superpower is on a far higher plane than being a nuclear superpower. But this kind of revolutionary step cannot be taken on a bilateral basis. It is possible only on a unilateral basis. Nuclear disarmament is not simply an act of destroying nuclear weapons. Nuclear disarmament, in actuality, is to turn a 'violence bomb' into a 'peace bomb'. It would bring about a peaceful explosion. Any nation that proves bold enough to take this peace initiative would apparently lose its status of nuclear power. But at the same time, it would gain a far more elevated status— that of a moral or spiritual superpower. Only such a superpower can meet the need of the hour, which is to initiate the process of peace. Only this peace 'explosion' can transform a world overflowing with violence into a world where peace reigns supreme.

Peace—Positive Behaviour

Peace is a product of a positive mental attitude, while violence is the result of a negative thinking. Peace is the natural state of society: violence is an unnatural state. Peace is as much in accordance with nature's plan as violence is against it. When peaceful conditions prevail in a society all activities take place in their proper form. But if the atmosphere of peace is disturbed, the normal functioning of society is disrupted. This law applies to man, as well as to the entire universe. According to the scheme of nature, peace is the only secret of smooth functioning in human society as well as in the rest of the universe. Peace, therefore, is such a basic requirement of man, that it is crucial to maintain it in all situations. Without peace there can be neither development nor progress. No excuse whatsoever justifies the use of violence, in individual or national life. Regardless of how unfavourable circumstances might be, an environment of peace is indispensable. We must maintain peace unilaterally, for nothing that we desire can be achieved without it.

If we fail to establish peace, then we must face destruction in every field of life. The option for us is not between peace and no peace, but between peace and annihilation. Without peace, there is no hope for the survival of mankind.

Spiritual Comfort

What disturbs the peaceful plan of nature is mainly traceable to the fact that people have become excessively materialistic. It is this thinking which leads to the exploitation of nature resulting in the disturbance of the peaceful plan of nature. If people opted for a path of moderation they would soon discover that, if earlier they were comfortable physically, now they are comfortable spiritually. And without doubt spiritual comfort is far better than material comfort.

The perpetrator of violence, be he a Hitler or a common man, invariably suffers from remorse, while the peacemaker derives great satisfaction from his efforts. If one were to think of the end result, one would never indulge in violence. One should bear in mind that peace is in consonance with humanity, whereas violence means a descent to the animal level.

Peace—Man's Absolute Right

Peaceful revolution is the outcome of peaceful thinking. Peaceful minds make for a peaceful world. Man was born in peace. Man must die in peace. Peace—man's birthright—is God's greatest blessing for human beings.

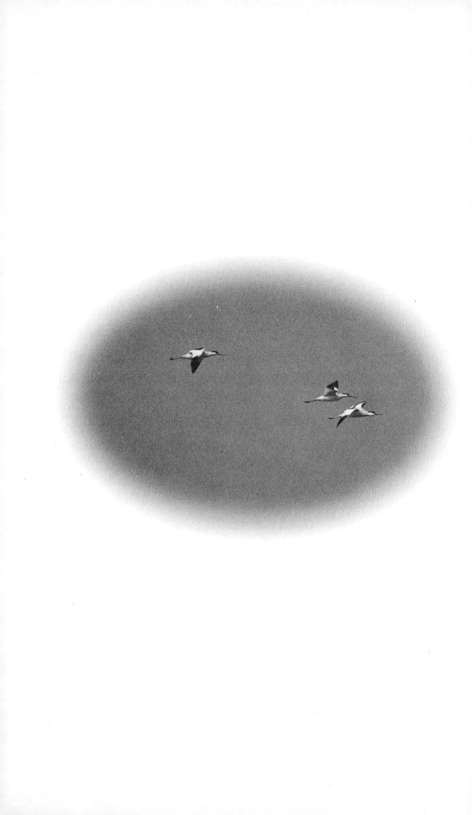

PEACE IN NATURE

A study of the universe shows that its all-pervasive system is based entirely on the principle of peace. There are innumerable celestial bodies throughout the universe, which are in perpetual motion. But no collision ever takes place between them. Each orbits with total precision within its own realm, never encroaching upon that of another, and that is why, in the world of nature, no clash or confrontation ever takes place.

The culture of the universe is the culture of peace. This is desirable for man too. Man also must adopt this all-embracing principle in his life. Renouncing the path of confrontation, he should opt for the path of peace.

Because of adhering to this peace culture, the universe has been functioning for billions of years without any such collision as would disturb its system. If a violent culture had prevailed instead, the different constituents of this universe would have collided and been destroyed. And the world would long have ceased to be inhabitable.

The Creator, who brought the cosmos into existence, also created human beings. It is His desire that man should likewise opt for the culture of peace that has been established in this vast domain. However, there is a difference between man and the universe. This peace culture has been imposed upon the universe by the force of nature. But man has been given freedom of action. It is desirable, therefore, that human beings should establish this peace culture by a conscious and voluntary effort of will so that harmony should also prevail in their lives.

The system of Nature

This earth, inhabited by man, has been properly set in order from the moment of its creation. For here, everything has been arranged according to a plan beneficial to mankind. This means that whatever man does on this earth, it is essential that he should do it without altering the plan of nature. If he tampers with it to even the slightest degree, it will result in the breakdown of the natural system already set in proper order and, in consequence, corruption will spread everywhere.

In our world innumerable events take place, governed by the law of nature: for instance, the continuous rotation of the earth, the receiving of light from the sun, the blowing of the wind, the onset of rains, the flowing of rivers, the growing of plants and trees, etc. All occurrences of this nature continue day and night. How striking it is that they occur in an extremely peaceful manner. There is no violence, no clash, no confrontation.

This being the natural way of reform, human beings ought to follow this way of nature, completely shunning violence and confrontation.

They should not conduct themselves like the violent individual who relies on things like swords, gun or bombs, but should draw their strength from noble human qualities, such as patience, forbearance, avoidance of conflict, a willingness for mutual adjustment, etc. These strategies of a peace-loving person are in conformance with the eternal and ineluctable laws of nature. Those who go against them will certainly create great disturbances everywhere; they will never be able to establish a reformed system.

The Law of Conversion

The human body requires blood in its system for its survival. But we cannot procure readymade blood in this world. For this we require a system where non-blood, after passing through a particular natural process, maybe converted into blood. Without this conversion, it is impossible to procure blood for ourselves.

Just as blood is vital for our physical existence, so is peace vital for our social existence. But we cannot find ready-made peace in this world. Therefore, in this matter as well, we will have to evolve a process by which non-peace may be converted into peace.

It is this peace-making process which was expressed by Jesus Christ in these words:

> "Give to Caesar what is due to Caesar and give to God what is due to God." (Luke, 20:25)

This means that, by avoiding a head-on clash with unfavourable circumstances, we may gain time for the achievement of our objectives.

In the context of peace this formula may be expressed thus: Tolerate the state of non-peace so that you may obtain the state of peace. This is the only way to convert non-peace into peace in this world. There is no other path to peace.

The entire system of nature is based on the principle of conversion. Everything in our world has undergone a process of conversion. Water, before being converted, had existed in the form of two different gases. According to the law of nature, non-water was converted into water. This process is applicable to all other phenomena of the world.

Let's take another instance – the tree. It never happens that a tree suddenly appears before us in its fully developed from. There is a process of nature, by which a seed is converted by stages into a tree. We can say that there is a process in nature, which converts a non-tree into a tree, then only a tree stands on the earth in all its majesty.

Similarly, a cow gives milk only after a natural process of conversion has taken place. It is as if the cow is an industry of nature, which converts non-milk into milk, a nutritious fluid. In a similar way, the food a man requires for his physical sustenance can come into existence only when nature's factory converts the non-edible into the edible, and man's digestive system further converts this edible material into flesh and blood.

The matter of peace too falls under this general law of nature. Peace is vital for our social existence but we cannot find ready-made peace in this world. Therefore, in like manner, peace can be had only by those individuals – or society – who have the ability to convert non-peace into peace. We can find peace only when we have demonstrated this ability.

Now let us see how this non-peace can be converted into peace. This process can be briefly summed up as giving a positive response in negative situations.

Our world functions on the principle of competition. That is why challenges and provocations are never absent from any situation. Our world can never be free from them. That sole remedy for this is to refuse to be provoked even in provocative situations. Peace is the result of such unilateral ethics.

In this world we can find nothing ready-made. Everything has to undergo a process of conversion. That is why we can never find ready-made peace here. We shall have to summon up all our wisdom to convert that which is not peace into peace. Only then can we possess peace. Just as this principle applies to the life of an individual, so also does it apply at national as well as international levels.

PEACE IN DIFFERENT RELIGIONS

Peace being the greatest concern of man, all religions attach importance to it. Indeed, peace is the essence of all religions, the reason being that the objectives of religion can never be fulfilled without peace. The aims of every religion, in principle, are man's spiritual development and the turning of each individual into a responsible citizen. This kind of education and training can never be imparted without a peaceful atmosphere.

Here, without going into too much detail, I would like to present briefly the teachings of various religions in this regard. (At the conclusion, Islam's concept of peace will be presented in a somewhat more detailed form, the reason being that in present times, violence is mostly spoken of with reference to the religion of Islam. It is widely believed that Islam justifies violence, whereas according to my study of the subject, this notion runs counter to the actual facts.)

Peace in Judaism

The history of Judaism goes back more than three thousand years. According to Jewish traditions, when the Israelites left Egypt and reached the Sinai desert, God

gave them the fundamental ten commandments that were
to govern their social existence. One of these was:

> You shall not kill. (Exodus, 20:13)

This biblical commandment forbids all kinds of
violence, whether individual or social, whether directed
against one's own community or against another. It was
revealed to Moses directly from God. According to Jewish
tradition this injunction is in the nature of an absolute
command.

There is another injunction of the Torah worth quoting
in this connection. It embodies such moral teaching as is
common to all religions, although differently expressed.
The wording of the Torah is as follows:

> What is hateful (or hurtful) to you, do not do to any other
> man.

In the context of peace, this teaching is very basic.
Obviously, we shall not find anyone in this world who
would like to be the victim of violence. Violence is
abhorrent to everyone. This being the reality, it is essential
that man should also abhor the perpetration of violence
on others. In no circumstances, should he indulge in
violent activities against others. Undoubtedly this
injunction is general in its application. It is addressed not
only to individuals but also to the community as a whole.
Just as a standard is set for individual behaviour, similarly
a standard is set for social behaviour.

Referring to this verse of the Torah, one Jewish scholar
has rightly observed:

"That is the whole of the Torah, the rest is but commentary."

In the Torah, Isaiah, an Israelite prophet, describes the world
of justice. In this most desirable world, "people shall beat their
swords into plowshares, and their spears into pruning hooks.
Nation shall not lift up sword against nation, neither shall
they learn war any more." (Isaiah 2:4)

This verse from the Torah shows that according to the
Jewish religion, the ideal human society is one where
people destroy their weapons; where war never takes place;
where the building of life is done on the basis of peace
rather than on violence.

This verse from the Torah is thus explained by a Jewish scholar:

"It is not enough merely to keep in mind the negative
admonition not to kill, but to transmute human energy and
efforts into peaceful and constructive actions."

Similarly, there is another verse from the Torah which
is worthy of mention. It describes the blessed
commandments of God:

"The wolf and the lamb shall feed together, the lion shall eat
straw like the ox, and dust shall be the serpent's food. They
shall not hurt nor destroy in all my holy mountain," says the
Lord. (Isaiah, 65:25)

In this quotation we are told in symbolic language
what the desirable society of God should be like. It is a
society where the weak and the powerful exist side by
side without harming one another; where the common
man enjoys the same rights as the VIPs. It is a society
where people can live peacefully without fearing any

injury from others; where people find in others, not violence but peace.

Peace in Christianity

Jesus Christ was born two thousand yeas ago in Jerusalem (Palestine). Today his followers are more numerous than those of any other religion.

The teachings of Jesus Christ are enshrined in the New Testament. They show that Jesus Christ laid the greatest emphasis on God-worship, love of human beings, service of mankind, spiritual development, rising above materialism, treating others well, even if they do not reciprocate, and so on. All these virtues, which in no way relate to war and violence, stem from the possession of a superior set of values. And all these values can be established in society by persuasion rather than by coercion.

The teachings of Christ in the New Testament tell us clearly that peace was so important to him that he enjoined the establishment of peace at all costs. In one of his sermons, Christ observed:

> Blessed are the peacemakers, for they shall be called the sons of God. (5:9)

This shows that, according to the teachings of Jesus Christ, the most blessed task is to establish peace in the world, peace in family life, peace in social life, peace in national life, peace in international life. The following observation of Jesus Christ is perhaps a realization of this peaceful world:

Your kingdom come – Your will be done on earth as it is in
heaven. (6:9)

In this quotation from the New Testament, what is
called the kingdom of God—can also be thought of as the
kingdom of Peace.

The teachings of Christ attach the greatest importance
to love and good behaviour. This is expressed in one of
his sayings in the Bible:

But I say to you who hear: Love your enemies and do good
to those who hate you. (6:27)

This means that you should love everyone, even your
enemies.

You should adopt a peaceful attitude towards everyone,
even towards those who choose to be physically abusive.
It is this unilateral good behaviour which has been thus
symbolically expressed:

To him who strikes you on the one cheek, offer the other also.
And from him who takes away your cloak, do not withhold
your tunic either. Give to everyone who asks of you. And from
him who takes away your goods, do not ask them back.
(6:29-30)

This is not encouragement to be passive. It is, in
symbolic language, a lesson in unilateral ethics. This
symbolic teaching can be expressed as follows: Establish
peace at all costs. Do not counter violence with violence.
Instead, counter violence by the unilateral exercise of
patience and the avoidance of conflict, in order that the
atmosphere of peace may not be disturbed.

Peace in Hinduism

Hinduism is based on the principle of non-dualism, which means that, in this world, the Creator and the Creation are not two different entities. It is rather the same reality which is manifested in different things and different beings in this world. According to this principle, a man and his fellow men are one and the same. There is no difference between one and the other.

This concept produces a sense of fellow feeling for all living beings. It negates the principle of otherness. Indeed, the feeling of otherness simply disappears. This being so, committing violence or aggression against others is, in principle, like committing aggression against one's own self. It is this concept, which is the ideological source of peace in Hinduism. The British historian, Arnold Toynbee, has called this a 'live and let live' concept of peace. That is, we should give peace to others and in exchange receive peace from them.

It was 2500 years after the establishment of Hinduism that Mahavir was born in a Hindu family in India. He laid down five principles of religion, and although the term 'non-violence' probably did not exist at that time in the ancient Hindu scriptures, the first and most important of these principles was *ahimsa*, which means non-injury. According to this principle, violence and aggression of any kind are absolutely wrong. Jain belief can be summed up in these words: The killing of a sensate being is a sin.

The Hindu religious leaders accepted Mahavir as their 24th avatar. In this way, the concept of *ahimsa* too became a part of Hinduism. In the 20th century too, there is the great example of Mahatma Gandhi, a Hindu reformer of world repute, who interpreted the Bhagwad Gita in the light of the principle of non-violence, and launched a full-fledged freedom movement entirely committed to this principle. The Encyclopaedia Britannica (1984) explains the degree to which Mahatma Gandhi was a pacifist: "Gandhi was the first to interpret *ahimsa* positively and in the sense of a social obligation." (13/847)

Tolerance is one of the basic principles of Hinduism

This concept of tolerance goes to the ultimate extent of encouraging belief in the truth of all religions. According to the Gita, each religious path leads towards the same destination: the truth. When Swami Vivekananda said, 'Every religion is true,' he correctly echoed Hindu belief. In Hinduism each religious tradition can be given equal recognition. Under the heading of 'Hinduism', the Encyclopaedia Britannica aptly states:

> "In principle, Hinduism incorporates all forms of belief and worship without necessitating the selection or elimination of any." (8/888)

This general concept of tolerance, in other words, instructs us to live in peace with others. One should not believe in adopting a violent manner towards anyone. Just as we regard ourselves to be right, we should likewise regard others to be right. In principle, violence against any human group is unlawful.

Peace in Buddhism

Buddhism is regarded as a godless religion, for unlike other religions, it does not entertain belief in God as a central concept. Instead, the Buddhist system is grounded on a set of moral principles. The basis of Buddhism may be called a moral philosophy, or an ethical way of life.

The life of Gautam Buddha (Siddharth Gautam), the founder of Buddhism, is historically not well authenticated, but it is believed that he was born in north India in 560 B.C. When he attained adulthood, he happened to see some scenes of human misery. Since he was a sensitive person, he began to ponder over the reason for pain and suffering. He then set himself the goal of ending pain and suffering in human life.

After a long period of deep reflection and meditation, he formulated certain moral principles. Since his chief objective in life was to end human misery, he attached the greatest importance to the fact that man should free himself from all kinds of desires. For it is these desires that lead man into all kinds of evils, including violence. The principles he set forth to govern human life are as follows:

> One must renounce all desires and all thoughts of lust, bitterness, and cruelty. One must harm no living creature. One must abstain from all killing. One must work in an occupation that benefits others and harms no one.

In principle, there is no place for violence in Buddhism. For the aim of Buddhism is basically personal reform. And personal reform can come about only by striving hard against one's own self, rather than by committing aggression against others. It would be correct to say that violence is something alien to the Buddhist scheme of things. Ideologically, Buddhism has no direct relation with violence.

PEACE IN ISLAM

THE QURAN is undoubtedly a book of peace. It is not a book of war and violence. This can be judged from the fact that all of the Quran's pronouncements are directly or indirectly related to peace. Its opening invocation is: "In the name of God, the Most beneficent, the Most Merciful" and this verse has been repeated in the Quran no less than 114 times. This is an indication that the greatest attribute of the Supreme Being who sent this book to mankind is mercy. Indeed, the theme of this entire holy book is God's all-embracing compassion.

The greater part of the scriptures, either directly or indirectly, strongly advocate peace. Of the 6666 verses of the Quran, there are hardly forty verses, which deal with the injunction to wage war, and then only in self-defence; that is, even less than one percent. To put it more specifically, only 0.6%.

Those who accept the Quran as the Book of God will be regarded as true believers only when they follow its admonitions and become peace-loving in the full sense of the word. Under no circumstances, should they launch themselves on violent courses of action. In order to conduct an objective study of this subject, it is necessary to differentiate between Islam and Muslims. Muslim action should not necessarily be seen as deriving from the teachings of Islam. In effect, Muslim practices ought to be judged by the criteria of Islam — which is an ideology — rather than Islam be judged by Muslim practices. Those who have abandoned the teachings of Islam can have no claim to be Islamic in their conduct, even if by their own lights they regard themselves as champions of Islam. Muslims are Muslims only when they follow the basic teachings of their religion.

Peace is God's name

The Quran puts on record the many names or attributes of God, one of them being As-Salam, that is, Peace. God loves peace and security so much that He chose Peace as one of His names. That is to say, that God Himself is the embodiment of peace.

Alkhattabi, has explained this verse in these words:

> "God is the Being from Whom all people feel safe and secure. From Whom people have the experience only of peace, not of violence." (Al-Qurtubi, Part 18, p. 46)

God has set the highest conceivable standards. That is, when God's dealings with human beings are based on peace and security, then man should also deal with other human beings in a peaceable manner, and not with harshness or violence.

No Extremism

In the fourth chapter of the Quran the following injunction has been given:

> "Do not go to excess in your religion." (4:171)

The same point has been made in a hadith. The Prophet of Islam observed:

> "You should restrain yourselves from committing excesses (*ghulu*) in religion. For it was due to their having gone to extremes in religion that the previous communities were destroyed." (Al-Nasai, Ibn Majah, Musnad Ahmad, 1/215, 347)

Ghulu means extremism. The way of extremism is wrong, whatever the circumstances, for it goes against the spirit of religion. Indeed, it is proneness to extremism which at times culminates in war and violence. Those who suffer from extremist tendencies remain dissatisfied with the path of moderation, since this strikes them as being far from the ideal. That is why they so easily incline towards violence, and are ever ready to open hostilities in the name of achieving their objectives.

Moderation, which is the opposite of extremism, is closely interlinked with peace. When people possess the virtue of moderation, they necessarily think in terms of peace and will engage in their struggle in a peaceful manner. Where there is moderation there is peace, and vice versa.

In stark contrast to this, an extremist attitude very soon leads to confrontation and violence. Extremism and violence are obviously interconnected. That is why extremism is held in religion to be abhorrent. It would not be wrong to say that violence is another name for extremism and that moderation is to refrain from extremism.

Killing one human being is like killing all mankind

The Quran states:

> "If someone kills another person, unless it is in retaliation for someone else or for causing corruption on the earth, it is as if he had murdered all mankind." (5:32)

Murder is a horrendous act. The killing of a human being is permissible only when the danger he poses to social peace has no other remedy. Killing a single person without proven justification is equal to killing all human beings. The difference between the two is only one of degree and not in nature. Killing one human being is just as horrendous as killing all human beings. Such a killing, without proper sanction, appears to be a simple matter. But such an act breaks all traditions of respect for life.

The above verse of the Quran shows the great importance of peace and security in Islam. If someone is unjustly killed, Islam demands that the whole of society should become so greatly agitated over this offence that it should work unitedly towards restoring a state of peace and security. It should be treated as a matter of the greatest of urgency, as if all of humanity were under attack.

Extinguishing the Fire of Violence

The Quran states:

> "Each time they kindle the fire of war, God extinguishes it."
> (5:64)

This verse of the Quran shows the creation plan of the Creator for this world — a plan based on the principle of peace. This means that whenever one of two opposing sides is intent on fuelling the fire of war, the other should attempt to extinguish it by resorting to some peaceful strategy, so that violence may be prevented from spreading. It should never happen that if one side indulges in violence, the other follows suit. The proper and most desirable way of leading one's life in this world is not to counter bombs with bombs, but rather to defuse them. And this should be done at the very outset. If we are imbued with the true spirit of Quranic teaching, we should realize that countering a bomb with another bomb is the way of Satan. On the contrary, the way approved of by God is to neutralize the bomb.

It is but natural for any given society to have to face distasteful situations. No group of human beings can ever be totally free from untoward happenings in their midst. This being so, the actual solution to the problem lies not in putting an end to the unpleasantness itself, but rather in refraining from aggravating matters, which is what inevitably happens if one kind of unpleasantness is met with another. Again, I would reiterate that bombs should not be countered with bombs. By refraining from violence, the baneful influence of social friction can be checked from spreading. There is no other possible solution.

War only for defence

The Quran states:

> "Permission to fight is given to those who are attacked because they have been wronged." (22:39)

This is not just a Quranic injunction aimed at Islamic believers, but rather a statement of international law. The above verse clearly states that war is permissible only when, in order to counter open aggression, it is waged in self-defence. All other forms of war come under the heading of aggression. And aggressors have no lawful place in this world. According to this verse, there is no justification for any war other than a defensive one, when one is compelled to do so.

According to the Quran, even defensive war can be fought only after making a formal declaration of war has been made, and then only by an established government (18:58). Non-governmental organisations (NGO's) have no right to wage war on any pretext. In view of these teachings, we can safely conclude that according to the laws of war stated in the Quran, all wars, except for a defensive war which has become unavoidable, are unlawful. For instance, guerrilla war, proxy war, undeclared war and aggressive war, all are undoubtedly unlawful in Islam.

War, in fact, is a bestial act. There is nothing human about it. Indeed, according to known and specific principles of Islam, peace is the rule, while war is only a rare exception.

Peace is something that can be opted for in all circumstances, whereas the decision to wage war should be taken only in times of emergencies for the purpose of defence, when it becomes inevitable, and that too at a time when all peaceful strategies for avoiding confrontation have failed.

Peaceful Persuasion, not coercion

On the subject of *jihad*, the Quran addresses the believers thus:

> "Do great *jihad* with the help of the Quran". (25:52)

As we know, the Quran is a book, an ideological book. It is not a gun or a sword. Therefore, '*jihad*' by means of the Quran can only mean conveying the ideas of the Quran to the people. This implies that we should struggle peacefully to make the ideas of the Quran understandable by presenting them in the form of logical arguments.

The above-mentioned verse makes it clear that what is called jihad in Islam entails only the kind of peaceful struggle which has nothing to do with violence. The Arabic word '*jihad*' is derived from the root '*juhd*' which means to strive, to struggle, that is, to exert oneself to the utmost to achieve one's goal. This is the original meaning of '*jihad*' in Arabic.

This verse shows that peaceful effort is vastly superior to violent effort. Whenever one opts for the violent method, the sphere of one's efforts becomes very limited. In resorting to violence, only the sword and the gun are of avail, whereas by peaceful methods, all kinds of things may be utilized to achieve our objective. Even a pen in a closed room can serve a great purpose.

Adhering to the truth with patience and perseverance

The Quran tells us that the kind of people who can save themselves from loss and achieve a successful life are those "who exhort each other to justice and to fortitude." (103:3)

It is unfortunate that one who adheres to the path of truth himself, or calls upon people to accept the truth is almost invariably rejected by the people. The resistance he has to face is very great. At such times what the lover of truth should do is exercise great patience. He should bear with fortitude all hardships, without trying to hold others responsible for it.

Patience is another name for the non-aggressive method. This means that one who stands up for the truth ought not to counter violence with violence. He must unilaterally adhere to peaceful ways.

Truth and violence cannot exist together. One who wants to opt for truth will have to abandon violence. Violence, whatever the pretext or justification, is still violence. All forms of violence are equally pernicious, and no elaborate justification of violence can nullify or diminish its destructive consequences. The ultimate weakness of violence is that it begets the very thing it seeks to destroy. Instead of diminishing evil, it multiplies it.

Perpetrating violence in the name of truth is the negation of truth. Those who engage in violence in the name of truth only prove that their case is not that of truth. A lover of truth can never be a lover of violence. One who loves violence is certainly not a lover of truth, whether or not he regards himself as a champion of the truth.

Adopting the Course of Reconciliation

During the times of the Prophet of Islam, as a result of the aggression of the Quraysh his opponents, a state of war prevailed between the Quraysh and the Muslims. One of the commandments given in the Quran on this occasion was:

> "And if they incline towards peace, you too incline to it, and put your trust in God. Surely, it is He Who is All-Hearing, All-Knowing. And if they intend to deceive you, then surely God is sufficient for you." (8:61-62)

This verse of the Quran shows that peace is desirable in Islam to the greatest possible extent. Even if peace can be established only by incurring risks, this course should unhesitatingly be embarked upon in the way enjoined by the Quran. If reconciliatory offers are made by the antagonists in the course of the war, they should be accepted without delay. Even supposing that there is the fear of some deception being practised in the making of the offer of peace, this offer should nevertheless be

accepted in the hopes that God will always be on the side
of the peace lovers and not on that of the deceivers.

Another reality that emerges is that, in this world,
peace can be established only by those who have great
courage. In the present world, problems inevitably arise
between different groups, for no human situation is ever
absolutely ideal. Everyone at some point in his life is faced
with injustice and the misappropriation of what belongs
to him by right. In these situations, only such individuals
can establish peace as can rise above all considerations
and disdain all pretexts to engage in violent retaliation.
Only the truly courageous can establish peace in this world.
Those who are lacking in courage will continue to fight,
and will thus never allow the history of the world to be
re-written in terms of blessed peace.

No Corruption on this Earth

In the following verse, the Quran alludes to a particular
kind of character, the self-styled reformer:

> When they are told, 'Do not create disorder on the earth,' they
> say, 'We are only putting things right.' (2:11)

This refers to those who claim to be engaged in reform
work, but whose method is of the wrong kind, for their
actions result in corruption and perversion. Here 'disorder'
(*fasad*) means that their activities result in clash and
confrontation with others, so that mutual hatred is
generated. In the process morality is undermined and a
negative mindset prevails. All these factors are referred
to as spreading corruption on the earth, for they all destroy

social peace, and ultimately, members of society are eternally at loggerheads with each other.

This teaching of the Quran shows that it is not enough for an action to have a good goal to be right. The kind of side effects produced by activities launched in the name of reform must also be examined. If these activities themselves produce tension and conflict—in spite of their goal being the laudable one of reformation—they would be regarded as spreading corruption. The doers will be deemed criminals and not reformers or servants of humanity.

No reform work is truly such, unless it is confined to the sphere of peace and humanitarianism. Any work, even if it is carried out in the name of reform, is to be condemned if it disturbs the peace, or worse, results in the loss of lives or the destruction of property. The task of reform should result in reform. If it results in social upheaval (fasad)) then this reform movement is in itself a form of societal perversion, irrespective of whatever fine words we may find to describe it.

The Greater Provision

A principle of life has been thus stated in the Quran:

> Do not regard with envy the worldly benefits that We have given certain of them so that We may test them. Your Lord's provision is better and more lasting. (20:131)

The truth is that there are two very different ways of living one's life. The first is entirely directed towards the material world. One who seeks success in terms of worldly

wealth and honour will find that there is no end to his
ambition. For if he sets purely worldly goals before him,
he will always find that there are people around him who
have more than he has. There is no escaping these
disparities. Therefore, one who lives for material things
suffers a perpetual sense of deprivation. This produces
feelings of discontent and jealousy, which surface again
and again in the form of rivalry, revenge and the
accompanying violence.

The second way for the individual is to lead his life
with a sense of achievement. Such a person will be content
with himself. This feeling of achievement will prevent him
from nurturing hatred against others or engaging in
violence. Who are those who are blessed with this feeling?
In the words of the Quran, they are those who are the
recipients of God's provision. God's provision means the
conviction of having discovered the truth: that the
existence they have been blessed with by their Creator is
more precious than all the world's treasures of gold and
silver. Each individual should, therefore, lead his life with
a keen awareness that the source of his intellectual and
spiritual nourishment is the entire universe.

One who becomes a recipient of God's provision in
this world rises so high that material things like wealth
and power become insignificant to him. This psychology
of its own turns him into a peace-loving person. Hatred
and violence appear to him so meaningless that he has no
time for such negative emotions or for making plans to
engage in violence. One who has found something greater

can never seriously pursue something smaller. He would therefore never engage in violence.

The prompt silencing of complaints

The complaining mentality is an aggressive one, which stifles positive thinking. It is the resultant negative thought which is undoubtedly the root cause of all evil. In most cases, it gives rise to the permanent sense of grievance, real or imaginary, which underlies any violence which takes place.

The creation plan in this present world has been devised in such a manner that there is no escape from grievances. This being so, the moment the thought of complaining first takes shape in the mind, it should be immediately dismissed. The complaint, if constantly recalled or revived, becomes so entrenched in the memory that it can never be thrust aside. In such a situation, wisdom lies in nipping complaints in the bud. Failing this, complaining will gradually become a permanent part of one's psyche, and then one's thinking will acquire a negative character. Others, will appear as enemies. Given a chance, the complainant will not then hesitate to engage in violence against the targets of his complaints, even if he himself suffers in consequence.

What is the formula for putting an end to complaints at the very outset? It is to give serious thought to the following verse of the Quran:

> And whatever misfortune befalls you, is due to what your own hands have wrought. (42:30)

This means that whenever we have any cause for complaint against anyone, we should direct it first at ourselves. We should try to explain it in such a way that the blame falls upon us. When we come to understand that we, rather than others, have made some mistake, we shall then set about rectifying our own shortcomings, rather than waste time in making protests and complaints against some supposed enemy.

A Mercy for Mankind

The Quran has this to say of the Prophet of Islam:

> We have only sent you as a mercy to all mankind. (21:106)

The advent of the Prophet of Islam made manifest God's mercy for all mankind. Through him God communicated those principles of life by opting for which man may inhabit the abode of eternal peace and security. (*Dar as Salaam*) (10:25). Through him, such teachings were revealed as would turn human society into a peaceful society. For the first time in history, the Prophet of Islam presented a complete ideology based on the concept of peace. He gave us the formula for the building of a healthy life, by shunning hatred and violence. Through him a revolution was set in motion, which made it possible to construct a peaceful society by avoiding war and confrontation. Although the Prophet of Islam was compelled to wage several battles, they were so brief that we might describe them as skirmishes rather than full-scale war. It would be quite correct to say that the Prophet of Islam initiated a revolution which, although very great in its scope and repercussions, was nevertheless almost bloodless. He gave peace the status of a complete ideology or system of life. He impressed it upon his followers that violence was the way of destruction, while peace was the way of construction. He held patience to be the greatest form of worship, implying as it does adherence to the path of peace in the full sense of the word. He held disturbing the peaceful system of nature (*fasad*) to be the greatest crime.

The Prophet enjoined believers to greet one another by saying *Assalamm-o-Alaikum*. This shows that mutual relationships should be based on peace and security. The Prophet told the believers that success in the Hereafter should be the target of the human struggle. In this way he dispelled the notion that worldly progress should be one's aim in life, for that is what ultimately results in all kinds of confrontation and violence. His formula for better living was to make oneself useful to others, and if that was not possible, then at least to do others no harm; no one should be regarded as an enemy; even the enemy must be given fair treatment, for only then would the realization come that one's enemy was potentially one's friend: the 'enemy' always has it in him to be a friend.

Peace in all circumstances

The Prophet of Islam was a peace lover to the ultimate extent. His opponents repeatedly attempted to draw him into war, but on each occasion he avoided becoming entangled. However, sometimes in view of unilateral aggression, he had no option but to fight purely in self-defence, and for a limited duration. Badr is one such battle.

History shows that at the exact moment when the armies of both sides were standing ready for battle, the Prophet was visited by Gabriel, God's angel. He said to the Prophet: 'O Muhammad, God has sent you peace (*salam*)'. On hearing this, the Prophet of Islam replied:' God is peace, peace is from Him and to Him is peace.' (Al Bidaya was al-Nihayah, Part III, p. 267).

This incident shows that even at such a juncture, the Prophet of Islam was a peace-lover. Even in that extremity, his mind was free from feelings of hatred and violence: he was thinking in terms of peace and security and his heart throbbed with the desire for these beneficent conditions to be established in the world with the succour of God. The true man is one who can think of peace even in times of war, whose heart is filled with feelings of peace and well-wishing, even during emergencies on the battlefield.

This is no ordinary matter. In reality, this serves as the highest example of positive thinking. As we know, war is the most negative of all events. The Prophet, who was at the helm of affairs, was on the brink of war, yet the words that came to his lips were those of peace and security rather than of war and violence. This is indicative of the highest human virtue. The noblest human character is one who thinks of peace amidst violence and who can plan for reconciliation even in wartime.

Peaceful citizens

According to a *hadith*, the Prophet of Islam defined a believer thus:

> A believer is one from whom people are safe as regards their lives and property. (At-Tirmizi, An-Nasai, Ibn Majah, Musnad Ahmad).

There are two ways of leading one's life in society. One is to live peacefully among one's fellow men. The other is to keep quarrelling with others. According to this hadith, the way of the faithful is to live as peaceful citizens in society. No one should pose any danger to others' lives, property or honour. In no circumstances, should one take the way of violence.

How should life be led so that the members of a society remain safe and secure from others' injustices? It is to maintain the way of moderation, irrespective of there being causes for complaint. They should be able to bury their complaints in their own hearts instead of pouring them out upon others. A society in which such self control is exercised is one in which its members can enjoy a feeling of security. Indeed, a peaceful society is the ideal framework for positive human development. On the contrary, a society fraught with violence is an animal, not a human society. It can offer little hope of the realization of individual human potential.

The love of peace is a noble human virtue, whereas the love of violence brings the human being down from a high ethical plane to the level of brutishness.

No confrontation with the enemy

The Prophet of Islam one observed: "Do not wish for confrontation with the enemy, ask for peace from God." This means that if someone has become our enemy, we should not necessarily turn against him and start fighting with him. Despite his enmity, we should opt rather for avoidance of friction, so that conflict is effectively prevented.

'Ask for peace from God' means to adopt the way of peace instead of confrontation and secure God's succour for peaceful activities. A believer should not pray to God thus: "O God, destroy the enemy." Rather his prayer should be: "O God, help me to stay away from the path of violence and confrontation, in spite of the enmity of others, and help me to pursue the journey of my life along the path of peace."

This shows that according to the plan of nature, peace in this world is the general rule, while violence is a temporary necessity. Furthermore, this tells us that if an individual or a group is our enemy, the way of confrontation is not the only way to solve the problem. A better and far more appropriate method is to neutralize enmity through a peaceful strategy. The power of peace is far more effective and far more useful than the power of violence.

The peaceful method is the best

We learn from a tradition what the Prophet's policy was in general matters:

> "Whenever the Prophet had to choose between two paths in any problematic situation, he would always opt for the easier course." (Al-Bukhari)

If this principle of taking the easier option is looked at in the context of the violent versus the peaceful method, it would be true to say that the way of the Prophet in any given situation was to refrain sedulously from using violent methods in dealing with the matter at hand. The peaceful course, therefore, must invariably be taken. For there is no doubt about it, that the violent method falls into the category of the harder option, while the reverse is true of the peaceful method.

However, this is not simply a matter of easier or harder options. It means rather that in our general dealings, the peaceful method is invariably oriented towards producing positive results, while the violent method is merely an exercise in futility. The violent method not only fails to solve the problem, but it further aggravates and complicates it. In the hadith, the harder method implies taking a course which is strewn with obstacles. On the contrary, the easier method implies acting in a way which facilitates the achievement of our goal.

The Limits of Difference

On the one hand, the Prophet of Islam observed: "To say a word of truth to a tyrant ruler is a superior form of *jihad*."

On the other hand, there is another *hadith* according to which the Prophet observed: "One who finds in his ruler something which he dislikes should endure it with patience." Similarly, on another occasion the Prophet observed: "Listen to and obey your ruler, even if he flogs you on your back or he appropriates your wealth."

There appear to be two kinds of commandments in these traditions: on the one hand, we are enjoined to tell the ruler clearly if he is treading the wrong path, whereas the other *hadith* enjoins us to remain unilaterally patient and bear all injustice.

These are extremely important injunctions, which distinguish between the verbal communication of advice and the taking of a practical step. It is certainly desirable that if a loyal subject sees his ruler taking the wrong path, he should bring this to his attention by means of sincere advice and with an attitude of well-wishing. But as far as taking practical steps is concerned, he must totally refrain from doing so. He must differentiate between sincere advice and the politics of confrontation. He should make use of his lawful right to utter well-meaning words of advice, while totally refraining from political confrontation.

This underlying principle is extremely important. An atmosphere of violence is produced in society when its members launch confrontational movements directed against their rulers, with the aim of overthrowing them in the name of political reform. If, on the other hand, they confined themselves to verbal advice and refrained from controversial politics, society would always remain peaceful. It would never become a jungle of violence.

The virtue of flexibility

According to a tradition, the Prophet of Islam observed: "The believer is like a gentle plant. Whenever the wind blows, it inclines accordingly, and when the wind stops blowing, it again comes back to its upright position. In this way, it saves itself from the impact of the wind."

According to this tradition, there are two ways of behaving during a storm. One is to face up to it with total rigidity. The other is to be flexible and bend before it. We can put it differently and say, there are two ways of countering adversity: one by the peaceful method, the other by the violent method. God enjoins renouncing the violent method in favour of the peaceful method.

Violence is basically an ego-related problem. It is a provoked ego that creates almost all kinds of violence and disturbance. When one's ego is affected, it turns into super ego and the result is breakdown. It is inevitably those who suffer from egoism who choose to be inflexible in weathering life's storms. Conversely, it is the modest who, in the face of adversity, tread the path of peace. In this world of God, destruction awaits those who indulge in egoism, while success awaits those who conduct themselves with modesty. The same point has been underlined in a hadith:

> "One who chooses the way of modesty will be raised up by God."

So the secret of peaceful living is to sedulously avoid any ego clash taking place between individuals or groups. This is the only successful formula for establishing a peaceful society on a permanent basis.

Self-evident Proof

A three-day symposium was held in Washington under the auspices of the American University in February 1998. At its meeting on February 6, the writer delivered a speech on the concept of peace in Islam. One part of this speech is reproduced hereunder.

It is no exaggeration to say that Islam and violence are contradictory to each other. The concept of Islamic violence is so obviously unfounded that, prima facie, it stands rejected. The fact that violence is not sustainable in the present world is enough to demonstrate that violence as a principle is quite alien to the scheme of things in Islam. Islam claims to be an eternal religion and, as such, it cannot afford to have a principle in its scheme which at any time could be found unsustainable. Any attempt to bracket violence with Islam amounts to casting doubt upon the everlastingness of the Islamic religion.

A phrase like 'Islamic violence' is the same kind of contradiction in terms as 'pacifistic terrorism'. The truth is that all the teachings of Islam are based, directly or indirectly, on the principle of peace. While all Islamic objectives may be achieved in a peaceful atmosphere, there are no Islamic objectives which may be achieved in a violent atmosphere.

A JOURNEY
TOWARDS PEACE

I have been associated with the issue of peace directly or indirectly since 1950. In this connection, despite the pressure of various other activities I have participated in a number of peace conferences, in India as well as abroad. A considerable number of my writings have been published on this subject. Here I would like to refer to three international peace conferences held recently on the issue of peace, which I attended and to which I tried to make my contribution. All three, held under the auspices of the Nuclear Disarmament Forum, under the chairmanship of Mr. Andre Bykov, were participated in by highly educated people from different parts of the world.

The first conference in this connection was held from the 25th to 30th of July, 2001, at Kandersteg, a famous resort in Switzerland, its topic being, "How to make a nuclear free world." On this occasion, I presented a paper, which is reproduced hereunder.

Ladies and Gentlemen:
The theme of this meeting is the complex issue of nuclear disarmament which, at this stage in world development, it is both appropriate and imperative

that we discuss in forums of this nature. I am grateful, therefore, to the organizers of this conference for giving me the opportunity to share my views with you.

What strikes me as being of prime importance is to fully understand the reasons for the stockpiling of nuclear armaments. In my opinion, the principal reason is mistrust between men and between nations. The escalation of this mistrust has caused the proliferation of nuclear armaments, and an increase in other related activities. What I believe to be mainly responsible for this mistrust is the lack of spirituality in modern times. We have to work at removing this root cause, without which it will be well-nigh impossible to make any progress.

There is a well-known saying of Jesus Christ. He said, "Love your enemy." It means that one must love everyone — including one's enemies. This is the essence of spirituality and religion: love and compassion for one's fellow men. And if we are serious about wanting to remove or solve all the problems that mankind is facing, especially in matters relating to nuclear armaments and acts of violence, we must lay greater emphasis on the purely spiritual, and revive the true spirit of religiosity.

I would like to mention an example from Islamic tradition. We know that the Prophet of Islam was born in Makkah and later on migrated to Madina. In those days, there were some Jews living in Madina.

One day, as the Prophet was sitting outside with his companions, the funeral procession of a Jew passed by. At this, the Prophet stood up, whereupon one of his companions said,

> "O Prophet! It was the funeral of a Jew, not a Muslim."
> The Prophet replied, "Was he not a human being?"
> (Al-Bukhari)

This came directly from the heart of a truly spiritual man. A genuinely religious person always feels compassion for all men and women, and loves them all equally. But when we are lacking in spiritual and religious values, we tend to become frightened and distrust those around us. In this modern world, we are witness to the spectacle of people exploiting one another. It has become easier to exploit others than to love them. I think that this in part is the explanation of our present dilemma.

The most important thing for us to do then, first and foremost, is to engender in ourselves and in others a genuine spirituality. That is the only way to create a world order based on love and compassion, which would in turn lead to the establishment of international stability. Without such positive measures, it will be impossible to solve the problems of today.

Thank you

On the occasion of the international conference in Kandersteg (Switzerland) at the request of Mr. Andre Bykov, chairman Nuclear Disarmament Forum, I prepared a document on this issue. At the end of the conference this document was presented on July 30, 2001 at a function held in the historical city of Zug (Switzerland). This was subsequently published for general distribution. This document is reproduced hereunder:

Peace is essential for a better way of living—peace of mind, peace in the family and peace in nature. Today, in our modern, technological world, man apparently has access to everything he desires, but in the absence of peace, everything has been rendered meaningless. What is needed to redress the balance is love, compassion, tolerance, forbearance and the spirit of co-existence. Peaceful co-existence is the only way of existence in this world.

How can we attain peace? The formula is very simple. Take your share without usurping that of others. Fulfil your needs without depriving others of theirs. Satisfy your desires without thwarting others and fulfil your ambitions without denying others theirs. In short, solve your own problems without creating problems for your fellow human beings.

However, a peaceful life can be achieved only when human beings learn what their limitations ought to be. According to the Divine law, you can take from the world whatever will satisfy your need—not your greed. You may do business with others, but not at the cost of the family and society. In daily existence, you may lead your life by maintaining the social structure and tradition and not by destroying them. You have the freedom to lead your own life, but by caring in the process for the rest of your society and not by neglecting it. Resources may be utilized for the benefit of humanity, but not for purely exploitative purposes. You are free to use peaceful methods, but you are not entitled to use violent methods. You can make use of nature, but only by maintaining its balance: the equilibrium of nature must never be upset. You have the freedom to use nuclear energy for peaceful purposes, but not to manufacture destructive weapons. You are at liberty to nurture feelings of love and compassion, but not to give way to hatred and prejudice. You are free to fulfil your physical desires, but not by killing your soul, spiritually. In short, you have the freedom to enjoy life by sharing with others, but certainly not by eliminating them.

In the present world the root cause of most of our problems is traceable to our deviation from the model of nature. Nature around us serves as the best model for us to follow. All the dilemmas we are facing today arise because we have ignored the model of nature.

The stars and planets are in continual motion in their orbits, but they never collide with one another. This serves as an example to show man how to go on in life without coming into conflict with others. He should continue his onward journey towards his destination without disturbing the path of others. The sun is a wonderful model. It shows us how we should give life to others in a totally indiscriminating way. The tree is also a shining example to man, in supplying healthy and beneficial oxygen in exchange for harmful gases such as carbon dioxide. And just look at how the flowers spread fragrance to others, regardless of whether they are appreciated for it or not. A flowing stream is likewise a model when it irrigates the fields without expecting anything is return. Without the inculcation of these altruistic values among human beings, no meaningful life on Earth is possible.

In short, positivity prevails throughout Nature. Negativity just does not exist in the world of Nature. This teaches us the lesson that we should give a positive response at all times, even in the face of negative situations.

An exhortation to follow Nature's example is exactly what Christ expressed in these divine words:

> 'Our Father in Heaven! Hallowed be Your name, Your Kingdom come; Your Will be done on earth as it is in Heaven.' (Matthew 6:10)

The second conference on peace, under the auspices of the Nuclear Disarmament Forum, was held at Ashdown Park Hotel, London, from 18 to 21 September, 2001. As an invitee to this conference, which was attended by delegates from different parts of the world, I made a speech during the deliberations. The text of this speech is reproduced hereunder.

Speech at London Conference

I am grateful to the organizers of this conference for giving me the opportunity to attend this international meeting, so that I may share my views with this learned audience. We started our journey of peace from Switzerland, where we successfully identified the basic problems faced by the world of today.

The joint declaration issued at the Swiss City of Zug called for the building of a better world, based on moral and spiritual values. For this to become a reality, peace had first to be established, for without peace no constructive work could be effectively carried out. It was emphasized that the beginning of the peace process would necessarily entail the elimination of nuclear weapons, without which no progress could be made.

One aspect of the deliberations in Switzerland was that the importance of ideology for stemming violence was stressed. Violence always begins in the mind, so we have to uproot it from the mind itself. We have to find an ideology of peace with which to confront the ideology of violence. Otherwise there will be no end to violence. The horrendous events in New York and Washington on September 11, 2001, are adequate proof of this point. They effectively demonstrated that, with a violent bent of mind, man can wage a war without even being in possession of arms. He can bombard without a bomb. Therefore, we have to eradicate the violent mindset and inculcate instead a peaceful way of thinking.

In view of this fact, and in the spirit of the Zug declaration, I have prepared two pamphlets titled *A Manifesto of Peace* and *The Road to Paradise*. This is my humble contribution to this universal mission. The first work describes the importance of external peace, while the second describes the importance of internal peace. Both are essential for a smooth and balanced development.

Now, I should like to make a few brief comments on the present team. This group of concerned people, organized under the dynamic leadership of Mr. Andre Bykov, seems to be a minority group at present, but being a small group or a minority group is not a minus point. As Schumacher has rightly said, "Small is beautiful." And the British historian, Arnold Toynbee, after a life-long study of history, tells us that it was those minorities who proved to be creative minorities who brought about the great revolutions of human history. I sincerely hope that this team will stand the test of creativity and will succeed in bringing about the revolution the world has been waiting for so long.

In conclusion, I would like to say that the formula for revolution is very simple:

> Change yourself and you will be able to change the whole world.

May God help you to realize this noble cause.

Nuclear Disarmament Forum,
Ashdown Park, London
September 14, 2001

The third international conference, under the auspices of the Nuclear Disarmament Forum, was held on October 12, 2002 in the historic city of Zug, Switzerland. This conference, in which I participated, was also attended by scholars from different parts of the world. I prepared a paper to present on this occasion, expressing my views on universal peace. This paper is reproduced hereunder:

The Beginning of a New Era

Nuclear Disarmament Forum, Switzerland   October 12, 2002

A historian has rightly said that the history of mankind is little less than a register of wars and violence. After the second world war this situation reached its climax. Now the world has witnessed the emergence of two super powers, both armed with thousands and thousands of nuclear bombs. But it was soon discovered that nuclear arms were practically useless due to their boomerang effect. Now it is generally accepted that nuclear bombs are useful neither for offence nor defense. And while using them brings about the annihilation of enemies, it is equally a suicidal course for the attacker. After this reality dawned upon the superpowers, nuclear bombs became for their owners a liability rather than an asset.

This realization led to serious negotiations between the two superpowers in order to put an end to this deadly menace. All minds sought a formula for the bilateral destruction of nuclear weapons. But this kind of bilateralism proved to be impractical.

By the grace of God, after long contemplation, I found the answer to this question, in a universal teaching of religion. This teaching was based on the principle of unilateral ethics, the application of which requires one superpower to start destroying its pile of nuclear weapons without insisting that it be done on a bilateral basis. Such unilateral action on its part would create a compulsive atmosphere for the other party, which would then feel that it had no option but to follow the same course, for it would then lose the justification for keeping its nuclear arsenal.

I first made this suggestion of following a unilateral policy at the international meeting organized by the Nuclear Disarmament Forum held July 26-30, 2001, in Kandersteg (Switzerland).

This idea was greatly appreciated by Mr. Andre Bykov, the Chairman of the Nuclear Disarmament Forum. I later compiled it in the form of a booklet and published it. At the next meeting of the Forum held in Ashdown Forest (England) in September 2001, it was distributed to all the participants. With the active support of Mr. Andre Bykov, this idea of unilateralism has been rapidly gaining ground.

It is a matter of great pleasure and satisfaction that Russia has already started to destroy its nuclear armaments. Thus Russia has become the first in the history of nuclear armament to begin the process of disarmament by disposing of about 100 kg of plutonium from surplus nuclear weapons, the equivalent of 10 atomic bombs, i.e. weapons having 100 times the detonating power that devastated Hiroshima. No doubt it is a decisive step towards destroying and disposing of weapons-grade plutonium worldwide. Although this process is now being liberally funded by the U.S.A., the credit for taking the first step must go to Russia.

Mr. Andre Bykov, an eminent Russian scientist, has successfully discovered a formula to extract plutonium from nuclear bombs, to be re-used for constructive purposes. By this formula, he has successfully converted destructive weapons into constructive machines. This is a really great and historic achievement. He deserves to be given the credit for saving humanity from nuclear conflict. And at the same time he has established that the human mind has a unique capacity to turn a minus into a plus. May God shower his choicest blessings upon him.

Now it seems that the dream of humanity is going to be fulfilled. The dream of a nuclear free world is going to be realized within a short period of time.

If the 20th century was a century of war and violence, the 21st century, it seems certain, is going to be a century of peace and happiness. A new world is being born. Mankind is once again on the threshold of a new era.

Now I would like to congratulate Mr. Andre Bykov for having successfully initiated the process of nuclear disarmament. It is a great international achievement to his credit.

It is a matter of great satisfaction that we have found a highly practical formula for avoiding the nuclear war which for a long time cast its shadow upon humanity. But

I would like to take this opportunity to point out that there is also another field which we have to consider in connection with this peace mission—that of terrorism. That is, armed action by private groups and individuals. And let us not forget that where a super power canot afford an endless war, terrorists can. These terrorists are people of a different breed: their ultimate goal is not necessarily victory. Death is also a desired goal for them. According to their self-styled ideology, they believe tht if they die in their militant struggle, they will instantly enter paradise. According to their beliefs, therefore, both victory and defeat have an equal value for them. In either case, they believe that they are the winners. Because of this unique ideology, these terrorists can continue their militancy for an indefinite period of time, generation after generation. But they are not a people apart. They are an integral part of their own whole generation. One of their great strengths is that the militants have an ideological factory for brainwashing their youths. This brainwashing process goes on unceasingly, and there is always a long queue of those who want to be recruited and be martyred.

Modern terrorism is thus a great and ongoing menace to our civilized world. Some powers of the world are engaged in crushing it militarily, but military action alone will not suffice to eliminate this phenomenon.

The reason for this is that present-day terrorism is actually militancy supported by an ideology. So it is not simply an issue of gun-versus-gun. It is, in fact, an issue of gun-versus-ideology. A bomb can be countered with a bomb. But an ideology cannot be countered with a bomb. For this we require an ideology of peace. So we have to formulate such an ideology as will banish the notion that there can be anything acceptable about terrorism. This would call for total mental re-conditioning of the terrorists. That is, we have to rid the minds of the militants of the ideology which is activating them. This, in effect, would be like defusing a bomb. With this very purpose in mind. I have published three books, called *The True Jihad, Islam and Peace and The Ideology of Peace*, which aim at persuading Muslim extremists to accept more peaceful solutions. After our successful experience of nuclear disarmament, we must now proceed to open a front for the ideological neutralization of the threat of terrorism. I hope we shall be successful in undertaking this most urgent task.

AN INTERNATIONAL
PEACE CENTRE

ESTABLISHING peace has become our first priority. Indeed, it is our greatest need, present-day circumstances having made it a crucial factor in human survival. But simply publishing appeals in support of peace or bombing terrorist hideouts is not the way to establish it. The truth is that the terrorism of the present age is different from that of former times. It is not a matter of who has the more sophisticated, and therefore some lethal technology. It is more a matter of technology versus ideology, for terrorism has a complete ideology—of its own making—to support it. Not until this ideology is destroyed can terrorism be rooted out. It will persist in one form or another.

Because of the undeniable seriousness of this problem, it has become essential that a full-fledged international peace centre be established at some focal point. This centre will aim at uniting peace-loving people the world over. Through literary efforts and by other means it will promote peace. Most important of all, it will bring to the people a sustainable ideology of peace. By using the present wide range of modern communications, it will propagate the culture of peace at the universal level. It will eradicate the mentality which dictates that violence must be countered with violence, and will highlight the importance of peace as opposed to violence.

This international peace centre will be like a peace factory where spiritual 'bombs' will be manufactured. And these spiritual bombs will rain peace all over the world in order that the global fire, set alight by violence and terrorism, may be extinguished.

The truth is that if it had been possible to put an end to modern terrorism by the power of the gun or the bomb, this would have already been done. The actual issue here is not how to put an end to modern terrorism by means of an armed struggle. Armed force has already been used on a large scale, yet the menace of terrorism has not been uprooted. Therefore, there is no question of repeating this futile exercise. Rather the question is that of changing our strategy to counter terrorism in the light of past experience.

This change would mean that peaceful 'bombs' should be used in place of violent bombs. The international peace centre will then function as the universal factory which produces these peaceful or spiritual ' bombs'. To be truly effective, it should be an entirely non-political and non-military organization. Any kind of political or military interference would be counterproductive. The objective of peace can be achieved only through peaceful means. The achievement of the objective of peace is just not possible by violent means.